Industrial Poverty

To my dear friend Susan W. Gore

Industrial Poverty

Yesterday Sweden, Today Europe, Tomorrow America

SVEN R. LARSON
Wyoming Liberty Group, Wyoming, USA

Routledge
Taylor & Francis Group

LONDON AND NEW YORK

First published 2014 by Gower Publishing

Published 2016 by Routledge
2 Park Square, Milton Park, Abingdon, Oxfordshire OX14 4RN
711 Third Avenue, New York, NY 10017, USA

First issued in paperback 2016

Routledge is an imprint of the Taylor & Francis Group, an informa business

Gower Applied Business Research
Our programme provides leaders, practitioners, scholars and researchers with thought provoking, cutting edge books that combine conceptual insights, interdisciplinary rigour and practical relevance in key areas of business and management.

British Library Cataloguing in Publication Data
A catalogue record for this book is available from the British Library

Library of Congress Cataloging-in-Publication Data
Larson, Sven R., 1965-
  Industrial poverty : yesterday Sweden, today Europe, tomorrow America / by Sven R. Larson.
      pages cm
  Includes bibliographical references and index.
    ISBN 978-1-4724-3932-1 (hardback) -- ISBN 978-1-4724-3934-5 (ebook) -- ISBN 978-1-4724-3933-8 (epub) 1. Economic development--Europe. 2. Financial crises--Europe. 3. Welfare state--Europe. 4. Europe--Economic conditions--21st century. 5. Europe--Economic policy. 6. Europe--Social policy. I. Title.
  HC240.L275 2014
  338.94--dc23
                                                                      2014010844

ISBN 13: 978-0-415-78965-3 (pbk)
ISBN 13: 978-1-4724-3932-1 (hbk)

Contents

List of Figures

List of Tables

Author Biography

Sven R. Larson, Ph.D., is an economist with a life-long interest in the tension between the welfare state and economic freedom. His doctoral thesis, *Uncertainty, Macroeconomic Stability and the Welfare State*, published by Ashgate in 2002, explored the role that government could serve in mitigating macroeconomic uncertainty. Since then, Larson has published numerous research papers and two more books, focused on various aspects of the welfare state, including comprehensive entitlement reform, single-payer versus market-driven health care, the relation between tax-paid entitlements and efforts at balancing budgets, and the social consequences of a welfare state in crisis. Schooled in the tradition of Post-Keynesian Economics, Larson appreciates traditional theoretical boundaries as a tool for learning and analytical rigor, but also finds them confining in the application of economics to practical policy solutions

Foreword

Europe's economic crisis has faded from the headlines. A combination of post-recession recovery and bailouts from international institutions has removed — or at least postponed — the potential for an immediate default or general economic meltdown. Besides, both the media and the American public have a limited attention span.

But that hardly means that it has gone away. Consider: the Greek, Irish and Portuguese governments alone owe some €717 billion (roughly $966 billion). Spain owes more than those three combined, €922 billion, while Italy and France each owe more than €1.85 trillion. All told, EU countries owe more than €11 trillion. And, that is just the debt that is on the books. If one includes the unfunded liabilities of their pension and health care systems, Europe is well over €100 trillion in debt.

Therefore, this new book by Sven Larson is both timely and important. In particular, Larson's thesis that the welfare state itself has damaged European economies and helped precipitate the recent recession is a message that today's policy-makers should pay careful attention to. There is an extensive body of public policy research showing that big government and large entitlement systems are bad for economic growth and prosperity. As Harvard's Robert Barro found, there is a "significantly negative relation between the growth of real GDP and the growth of the government share of GDP." In other words, as government spending goes up, economic growth goes down. This is especially true with transfer payments and other non-investment spending.

But there are still important gaps to be filled in our understanding of the systemic role of big government and the welfare state. The Great Recession is a good example of such a blank space. Some of those questions are concerned with the financial system and whether or not over-regulation and other government interference with the financial industry exacerbated — or even caused — the global financial crisis. But some questions also center on what role the welfare state played in the crisis. Based on what we know generally about the negative role of big government in the economy, it is important to ask whether or not the welfare state had anything to do with the cause, the depth or the length of the crisis.

Larson provides convincing evidence that the welfare state, and misguided policy choices by Europe's governments, turned a regular recession into a systemic economic crisis. During the seemingly prosperous first years of the European Union, few people could foresee the problems ahead, and even fewer viewed these developed countries as struggling with a form of poverty. However, during this stubborn economic recession, GDP growth in many European countries slowed (or even stopped), private consumption stalled, government spending surged, and unemployment rates among the young increased. This book helps us to better understand the current situation facing Europe today, one far more complicated than the *austerity versus stimulus* dichotomy that is so often imposed.

Larson argues that many of the austerity measures pursued in Europe have done little to address the true causes of the recession, a structural crisis that the large and unwieldy welfare state is largely responsible for. This structural crisis is comprised of three parts: a fiscally unsustainable welfare state, the high taxes needed to pay for it, and work-discouraging entitlements that depress labor force participation and lower economic activity. Part of the problem with responses to the recession was a hesitation to recognize that this was not a "normal" recession, and that structural reforms that significantly alter the welfare state might be needed.

He acknowledges that if it is well-designed and actually implemented, austerity can improve the budget outlook while also improving the economy. However, austerity, as it has been enacted in Europe, has been focused on the short term, with spending cuts, tax increases and budget gimmicks that are an attempt to "recalibrate" the welfare state; for the most part, these are attempts to make the welfare state more affordable, rather than pursue substantial and structural reform. By slimming down the welfare state, these countries are resigning themselves to a less active economy, slower growth and lower prosperity. Indeed, the real concern is that these countries will be resigned to "industrial poverty," a situation Larson describes in accessible, testable metrics.

In industrial poverty, the basic needs of a country's citizens are met, but the economy is stagnant. In this situation, consumption does not grow, unemployment remains elevated and government remains oversized. Larson argues that these countries must look beyond just the balanced budget, and should expand their focus to economic growth, lower unemployment and smaller government. In their responses to the recessions, he proposes a framework in which these countries instead focus on reforms that roll back the welfare state in a structural, permanent way, rather than simply improving the budget outlook in the short term. These long-term, structural changes would limit economic uncertainty in the future and foster stronger economic performance, helping these countries to avoid the pitfalls of industrial poverty.

For the United States, Europe's crisis provides an extraordinary laboratory, enabling us to view the results once the modern welfare state becomes unaffordable. The instability being seen in Europe today presents the likely endpoint for this country unless we are able to put our economic house in order.

The United States has long been accustomed to an economy that grows faster than those in Europe. This is one reason why our unemployment rate has been much lower. However, if the United States ends up with a European-size government, we can expect to see slower European levels of growth, and much higher, European level, unemployment.

While the burden of government is lighter in the United States and the welfare state is less developed, recent developments like the implementation of the Affordable Care Act, declining labor force participation rates, and myriad of tax increases should raise concerns that the United States could also be trapped in a form of industrial poverty unless some steps are taken.

The United States faces a massively growing debt that threatens our economic future. But as bad as that debt is, it is merely a symptom of a larger disease: a rapidly growing government that is consuming an ever larger share of our national economy. As a result, the United States is well down the road toward a debt crisis similar to Europe's. That we haven't already experienced such a crisis is the fortuitous result of the United States' position as the world's reserve currency combined with the overall strength of our economy. But that will not protect us forever.

Unless the United States learns from the failure of Europe's welfare state and acts now to reduce spending, reform entitlements, and reduce the growing burden of government, we will eventually find ourselves in the same situation as Europe.

Michael Tanner
Senior Fellow, Cato Institute, Washington, DC

Preface

Why I Wrote This Book

This book is an exploratory endeavor. It asks a question that cannot be fully answered today, a question that may require many more years of inquiry before the answer is complete.

It is admittedly risky to ask a reader to spend the money, time and effort to read a book that already at the outset promises to leave him or her with new questions rather than with definitive answers. However, there are moments in time where the formulation of a problem and a first attempt at solving it can open new perspectives on our lives, our society and our economy.

The question asked in this book has to do with the deep, persistent and increasingly urgent economic crisis in Europe. Conventional wisdom would have it that this is a recession like others, only a bit more serious. I am not ready to accept that claim. On the contrary, I find several reasons to question it. For one, this recession is deeper, longer and more destructive than any other non-war crisis since the Great Depression. In some countries the crisis is now in its fifth year, with GDP being stagnant or even shrinking. Unemployment is at levels not seen since the 1930s, with no improvement in sight.

Furthermore, the remedies that established economists and political leaders have proposed and put to work have proven utterly ineffective. Instead of improving the economy, the policies deployed to fight the recession have actually aggravated the crisis. Greece, to mention one example, has lost 25 percent of its GDP since the crisis broke out in 2009—despite several years of repeated, concerted policy efforts to turn the economy around.

Other countries exhibit similar immunity to anti-recession policies. Spain, Portugal, Italy and France have all tried various versions of the same supposed cure: austerity. But the crisis has only gotten worse, with persistent budget deficits, stagnant or shrinking GDP and one-fifth of all young people being unemployed in 19 countries in Europe.

If the medicine is not working, it is time to ask if the diagnosis was correct in the first place.

I suggest that it was not correct. If designed carefully and correctly, austerity can have a positive effect on both the budget deficit and macroeconomic activity. The version of austerity implemented in Europe is of an entirely different kind. In fact, it is clear by now that austerity as the Europeans know it is exacerbating the crisis instead of curing it.

The reason is that austerity as designed in Europe has one short-term purpose: to save the welfare state by making it slimmer, so that it can fit into a smaller tax base. But this kind of austerity is built on the assumption that the welfare state is not the cause of the crisis, an assumption that is entirely wrong.

On the contrary, Europe is suffering from a structural crisis, caused in large part by the welfare state. The crisis will remain for as long as the welfare state exists.

Again: the reason why Europe is not getting out of its crisis is that its governments are trying to save the very root cause of the crisis. With various combinations of tax increases and spending cuts, European governments are trying, year after year, to recalibrate the welfare state. Their hope is that higher taxes and less spending will balance government budgets at a lower activity level and thus make the welfare state fit within a tighter tax base and a less active economy.

Austerity as put to work in Europe today has nothing to do with reducing, let alone eliminating, the welfare state.

Conceivably, the hope has been that when the economy recovers (again under the erroneous assumption that this is a normal recession) the calibration of taxes and spending in the welfare state could return to "normal" rates. But for the time being their goal with austerity has been to be able to continue to deliver the entitlements of the welfare state when fewer people are taxpayers and more people demand its service.

The problem is that since this is not a normal recession, the economy does not respond well to this kind of policy. Instead, the result of this recalibration of the welfare state is that the government takes more from the private sector and gives less back. Inevitably, this imposes a new, tougher burden on the private sector, resulting in a depression of both government and private-sector activity.

The error in the economic diagnosis lies in the combination of two presumptions. The first is that Europe was equipped to meet a regular economic recession, something that is highly debatable if not entirely false. Europe was exhibiting clear signs of economic stress in the years leading up to the recession.

The second presumption is that Europe could go into the crisis and still afford its welfare state. The large government deficits across Europe present evidence to the contrary; so long as the welfare state remains in place without substantial reforms, and in fact becomes more of a burden on the private sector by means of austerity, there is no chance of a recovery in the European economy.

In short: the European crisis is structural in nature and therefore requires a structural response. Europe's lawmakers cannot use policies aimed at preserving an intact welfare state, but should instead focus on reforms that return critical economic territory to the private sector.

There are three elements to the structural crisis:

- a fiscally unsustainable welfare state;

- the high taxes needed to pay for it; and

- work-discouraging entitlements.

Together, these three elements depress private consumption, dissuade business investments and slow down economic growth.

To end this crisis, Europe's political leaders will have to put to work an entirely different kind of spending cuts than what they have tried thus far. The design of these new cuts starts with a new motive: instead of attempting to keep the welfare state structurally intact, Europe's governments must implement permanent reforms that substantially reduce the welfare state's presence in the lives of Europe's citizens and businesses.

But spending cuts alone cannot rescue Europe: what is needed is an entirely new combination of economic policy measures, based on a synthesis between two seemingly incompatible paradigms.

Before we develop this new synthesis we first need to analyze the nature of the European crisis. This analysis begins with the recognition that austerity as currently applied to Europe's economies is fiscally ineffective and socially harmful and that it has in fact exacerbated the crisis.

We also need to understand the deep and profound consequences of staying on the present course. It is not an exaggeration to say that the current crisis is a transition from one "normal" to another. Europe is abandoning its position as a first-world, well-to-do continent, descending into what is best described as industrial poverty.

This transition did not come about unannounced. Europe has been showing signs of economic stagnation for at least a decade. Private consumption, the largest part of GDP, has been almost flat since at least the Millennium Recession. This is a clear sign that middle-class families no longer experience a rise in their standard of living over time.

Other variables, such as youth unemployment and government budgets, have also been in trouble over a long period of time. It was inevitable that a major, structural crisis would surface.

An aggravating circumstance is the increasing imbalance between private and public sector economic activity. Over the past 50 years, every single European country has raised taxes, often significantly. Government is now consuming more than 40 percent of the economy in almost every EU member state, and the trend is still upward.

During the recession this long-term burden conspired with persistently high unemployment, permanent depression of private consumption and the wrong kind of economic policies. This unintended conspiracy began the transition from one "normal" to another; from a Europe in prosperity to a Europe in industrial poverty.

This is my hypothesis of what Europe is currently experiencing. The purpose of this book is not to deliver the definitive answer to this hypothesis. It would be arrogant to make such an attempt while Europe is still in the middle of the crisis. The purpose is instead to define the premises of what I suggest is Europe's new normal and to lay out the foundation of an economic policy that could put Europe on a track to prosperity again.

Why America Needs to Pay Attention

The European crisis has taken proportions that are difficult to grasp from an American viewpoint. Yet it is critically important that American legislators, voters, taxpayers and policy-makers comprehend both the nature of the crisis and how easily the wrong kinds of crisis mitigation policies could bring it over to U.S. shores.

To put the European situation in perspective, consider the drastic 25 percent decline in Greek GDP over the past four years. In American terms a loss of one-quarter of GDP equals $4 trillion. Approximately, this translates into the loss of 32 million jobs.

Yes, that's right. Thirty-two million jobs.

A middle-class American family would lose up to $2,000 in income—per month. They would still have the same cost of living (though taxes would ostensibly be higher as a result of austerity). Their kids' schools would be worse; health care would be worse; crime would go up and police protection would be cut.

Entitlements would be drastically worse than they are today. Unemployment benefits would be cut below welfare. Medicare and Medicaid would force enrollees to pay full market price for medicines.

This is all happening in Europe. And it provides a chilling view of what would happen if we tried to use austerity to get rid of our big budget deficit. Our crisis is, namely, of the same kind. Our luck is to be a few years behind Europe, in a position where we can watch, learn what not to do and design a different path out of the crisis.

Like Europe, the United States has an elaborate welfare state with fewer differences than similarities with Europe; we have experienced a long-term recession; in recent years the economic crisis has brought our youth unemployment up to levels it has rarely been at historically; and we have a very large budget deficit.

At the same time, there are notable differences that so far have kept the European crisis from making landfall in the United States. Although there are good reasons to criticize tax policy in the United States, American taxes are not yet at European levels. We also do not have a general income security system of the vastly developed European kind, and even with the Affordable Care Act in place, our health care system is still a fair stretch away from the prevailing European single-payer model. While the private sector is undoubtedly struggling in the United States, its situation does not rise to the same level of severity as private businesses and households are experiencing in Europe.

Perhaps the biggest difference thus far into the current crisis is that U.S. fiscal policy has not yet resorted to European-style austerity. Herein lies the biggest reason for American legislators, voters, taxpayers and policy-makers to pay attention to the European experience: despite—or, as I shall argue in this book, because of—years of austerity, budget deficits across Europe are still staring lawmakers in the eyes, unfettered by harsh spending cuts and drastic tax increases. The United States can still choose a different path to a balanced budget, economic growth and restored prosperity.

Acknowledgments

First and foremost, I am indebted to Michael Tanner, senior fellow with the Cato Institute. On three occasions he generously and vigorously read and commented on the manuscript that eventually became this book. Mincing no words, Tanner exposed glaring weaknesses, challenged me to explain vague or unclear passages, and to elevate the analysis to yet another level. As humbling an experience as it was, the final product is vastly better thanks to him.

Tanner and I first got to discuss austerity and fiscal policy in a Facebook exchange about the Baltic countries. It gradually evolved into an e-mail exchange, a person-to-person conversation and more e-mail exchanges. We came into the discussion from widely different angles but gradually found common ground. That is not to say we agree across the board, but there is absolutely no doubt that I benefited vastly from our conversations and from his exercise of true, classic scholarship.

My wife, Christina, has also been a great source of inspiration and aspiration in the pursuit of this project. A journalist by profession, Christina's inquisitive mind and deep understanding of Sweden helped me bring clarity to an important case study in this book. I am also grateful for Christina's patience with my countless late-night sessions with the material for this book.

J.D. Foster, economist with the U.S. Chamber of Commerce, has been a valuable peer, helping me stay grounded and focused in the more intricate theoretical analysis. Always emphasizing the practical side of economics, Foster skillfully challenged me to concentrate on the useful and let go of the useless parts of economic theory.

Dan Mitchell, senior fellow with the Cato Institute, is another good friend and peer. Early on in this project he directed me to studies that contradicted some of my early conclusions regarding the European crisis.

It is safe to say that this project would not have become meaningful had it not been for the inspirational support from my dear friend Susan Gore. With her encouragement to think out of the box, she inspired me to go beyond what conventional thinking and standard analytical frameworks would have allowed.

Despite such great support, in the end a book can never be perfect. What remains of shortcomings, unanswered questions and other flaws are entirely attributable to the author.

Lastly, an acknowledgement of mentorship. Conventional research in economics applies rigorous mathematical methods, centered around advanced models. While such methodology is highly applicable to the problem areas explored in academic journals, it does not fit the kind of problem explored in this book. Throughout my academic training, from undergraduate through graduate, I had the opportunity to learn from economists whose own training in many cases pre-dated the transformation of macroeconomics during the 1980s. Thanks to their teaching I learned to analyze complex economic problems without the mainstream economist's problem-restricting reliance on formal models. In terms of quantitative reasoning, this book is limited to multi-step statistical analysis, based on several sources of raw data, combined with the application of standard macroeconomic theory. It is not my ambition to produce research that fits the requirements of regular academic economics; the first endeavor into a new analytical problem determines the choice of methodology, not the other way around.

Chapter 1

The Nature of the European Crisis

The prevailing opinion among economists, legislators and public policy scholars on both sides of the Atlantic Ocean tends to be that Europe is in a regular economic recession. This is evident from the policy response that the crisis has been met with. Understandably, an argument that suggests the crisis is in fact not at all regular, but unique and structural in nature, must come with compelling evidence. In order to rise to this standard, the following chapters present a three-step argument for a structural European crisis.

The first step presents evidence that the notion of a regular economic crisis is wrong. The second step defines industrial poverty in a form that is easily testable without the use of complex economic methodology. The testing method presents four criteria for industrial poverty.

The third and last step explains to what extent Europe meets those four criteria.

Starting with the first step, there is plenty of evidence that Europe's crisis is abnormal. This book is not the first outlet for such a suggestion, though other critics of the conventional wisdom on the crisis are few and far between. Among the few who seek an alternative explanation to the crisis, the best example so far is Olivier Blanchard at the International Monetary Fund. In a January 2013 working paper with IMF economist Daniel Leigh, Blanchard admitted that the IMF's macroeconomic analysis of Europe had not accounted for some of the unconventional properties of the crisis.[1]

Yet the resistance to accepting a new, structural explanation of the crisis goes deeper than what data can penetrate. Beyond the convenience of relying

---

1   Blanchard, O. and Leigh, D., *Growth Forecast Errors and Fiscal Multipliers*, Working Paper WP/13/1, International Monetary Fund, Washington, DC, 2013.

on conventional wisdom, there is also a deeper, cultural character trait in our modern societies that reinforces an intellectual bias against unconventional explanations of complex social and economic problems. This bias is particularly strong in our time because of the unprecedented rise to prosperity that, among others, Europe has seen over the past two centuries.

We, the children of the 20th century, were born into an era of unprecedented prosperity and steady progress. The modern world, we were told, would always get better and more and more people would share the proceeds of a growing, thriving economy. Engineers produced new inventions that made it easier and cheaper to clothe, house, feed and cure more people. Economists developed new policies that encouraged more entrepreneurship and created more jobs.

We discovered environmental problems, and gradually began finding solutions to them. We started recycling and buying organic food. We reduced carbon emissions, went to paperless communications and learned to live more efficiently.

We kept making progress. And we kept expecting progress. Like the evolution from the Atari desktop to the iPhone, we thought it was natural that we would constantly get more for less.

We were so caught up in our belief in steady progress that it seemed only natural to us that government would be part of it. Our politicians participated by promising more entitlements and more government programs for more people. To many, that seemed like a good idea. Since everything else was getting better, it was easy to assume that more government was better than less, without qualifications. We merrily accepted to let government give us health care and child care; it made sense, we thought, to let government educate our children.

We let government take care of the poor, feed the needy, clothe the deprived, house the desperate.

The welfare state seemed rational, modern, progressive. Everyone was going to get what they needed.

We, the children of the 20th century, were so caught up in taking progress for granted that we could not imagine that the train we were riding would ever come to a halt. We assumed that progress, technological and economic advancement were part of the natural order of modern society. All we had to do was enjoy the ride, pay our taxes and work 37.5 hours per week.

Throughout the era of modernity and assumed progress, there have been many voices raised against the welfare state and against a steadily growing government. But even among those who have been at the forefront of criticizing the gradual expansion of the welfare state there seems to be an implicit resistance to believing that our era of prosperity could indeed be coming to an end.

Yet the crisis in Europe calls on us to re-examine our beliefs in steadfast progress. The emerging story is that we are facing a crisis of an entirely new kind. Europe's ailment suggests that this is a crisis brought about by a welfare state that can no longer survive on whatever tax revenues the private sector can provide.

But the emerging story also tells us that in order to address the crisis, conventional policy measures will have to give way to more powerful, long-term policy solutions. The solutions required for the current crisis likely clash with established beliefs among economists as well as political leaders; with conventionally accepted dichotomies between economic theories; and with deeply established ideological paradigms.

At the heart of the challenge to commonly held beliefs is the fact that the welfare state no longer delivers as promised. It is a key element of the crisis that welfare states in several European countries are defaulting on some of their entitlement promises. The poor are getting poorer, hospitals are letting patients down. People lose their jobs, their homes and fall from comfortable middle-class living to a life in deprivation and despair—something that the welfare state was supposed to prevent.

In the midst of the most modern, most progressive, most rational of societies—the European welfare state—there is now widespread misery, hopelessness and apathy.

The crisis has brought into question the very existence of the welfare state. It would be wrong to conclude that if only the welfare state was removed today, the crisis would be over tomorrow. At the same time, the crisis has exposed as false one of the premises behind the welfare state, namely that there will always be more economic growth available to pay for ever-expanding government entitlements. The tax base that for decades has funded an increasingly generous welfare state can no longer be taken for granted.

Again, this is not front page news. Europe's political leaders have for a long time ignored the mechanisms that define a modern economy. They have not seen the message embedded in a slow but inevitable erosion of the welfare state's tax base. The noble cause behind the welfare state—to even out the distribution of income and to provide universal access to services deemed as essential—overshadowed economic realities.

Where a slowly growing tax burden and slowly expanding entitlements originally had no significant impact on private-sector activity, the modern welfare state of the late 20th century reached such proportions that it dissuaded productive private-sector activity. When the current recession began, Europe's welfare states had no margins of growth and employment to shield them from a genuine, structural crisis.

The current crisis suggests, rather sternly, that Europe's political leaders can no longer take for granted that the private sector can pay for the welfare state. Yet it is precisely the ignorance toward this suggestion that has led Europe's political leaders to the conclusion that the current economic crisis is just another recession. It was based on the false notion that the welfare state could survive the crisis without fundamental, structural reform that led them to borrow large amounts of money already before the current crisis came ashore with full force. From 2007 to 2011 Europe's governments sold a trillion euros worth of Treasury bonds to financial institutions just in order to keep funding their welfare states.

For lawmakers, this meant turning a blind eye to the writing on the wall. But politicians were not the only ones who thought the signs of macroeconomic ailment were just another recession in the making. The banks welcomed the abundant supply of Treasury bonds. In the years leading up to the current crisis, banks in both Europe and the United States were exposed to dangerously high-risk investments, especially in real estate. When the welfare states on both sides of the Atlantic Ocean accelerated their sales of Treasury bonds, banks saw a good opportunity to reinforce the low-risk anchor in their portfolios.

Initially, the banks got it right. They were happy to play along and apparently ignored emerging signs of a looming crisis in Europe's welfare state economies. Had 2008 and 2009 only been about widespread defaults on mortgage loans, the global financial crisis would likely have been contained. But the banks soon found themselves taking massive losses at the high-risk end of their portfolios while at the same time the Treasury bonds at the low-risk end were in jeopardy.

The crisis became acute when Greece ran out of cash and stood a few inches—or euros—from defaulting on its debt.[2] In 2011 banks that had invested in Greek bonds to balance their higher-risk loans were forced to write off up to 20 percent of their loans to the Greek government.[3]

Ireland and Portugal started having problems. The Spanish government's credit was downgraded. Even the credit status of the United States was questioned.

And so on. The bank crisis was catapulted from a problem of mortgage defaults to entirely new heights. The decline in bank solvency was a major sign that Europe's economic crisis was much more than what conventional wisdom would suggest. The banks that had suffered from speculative mortgage lending suddenly found themselves with frighteningly small portions of low-risk assets in their portfolios. Edging closer to default, they now asked governments for help. But by helping banks, the cash-strapped welfare states around Europe had to borrow even more money—or enforce even more destructive austerity.

Suddenly, the governments that were supposed to lead their nations toward new heights of prosperity and progress were playing desperate fiscal defense. The crisis took a chokehold on Europe's economies. Political leaders were taken by surprise as deficits opened up in government budgets. The policy response reflected the lack of preparation. Fiscal panic set in, austerity became the norm, leading legislators across Europe to make drastic, desperate cuts in welfare programs. They slashed their health care systems, cut pharmaceutical subsidies and raised college tuitions. They raised taxes.

Focused entirely on immediate deficit reductions, Europe's leaders added insult to the continent's macroeconomic injury. Desperate to root out the deficit and make sure the welfare state could continue to live, they found out that the government budget was immune to austerity. In response, the leaders of the EU and its member states doubled down on the same policies.

Taxes went up, government spending went down. Taxpayers paid more but got less and less for every euro they paid. In many euro-zone countries, GDP growth turned into GDP decline.

---

2   "Bank official: Bond bubble biggest threat to financial stability," *City AM*, June 13, 2013. Available at: http://www.cityam.com/article/bank-official-bond-bubble-biggest-threat-financial-stability, accessed December 27, 2013.
3   Eurostat, Government Finance Statistics. Available at: http://epp.eurostat.ec.europa.eu/portal/page/portal/government_finance_statistics/introduction, accessed December 27, 2013.

Progress turned into regress. Austerity jeopardized prosperity. Suddenly, things were not getting better. They were getting worse.

Greece was leading the downward spiral. By early 2013, the Greek economy had shrunk by a staggering 25 percent in four short years. Overall unemployment was 27 percent, and 60 percent among the young.

Portugal, Spain, Cyprus and Italy were not far behind Greece. Ireland, France, the Netherlands, even the Czech Republic got a taste of the austerity medicine. All over Europe life was suddenly getting tougher with each year, not better.

Things can get even worse, and if there is no change in policy, they will. Fortunately, some public policy scholars are catching the real character of the crisis. Notable among them is Michael Tanner, senior fellow at the Cato Institute:[4]

> *As government has taken responsibility for more and more areas of our lives – from retirement and health care to protecting us from unemployment or guaranteeing a minimum level of income – it has grown ever bigger, most costly, and more intrusive. At the most basic level, it has become unaffordable. Despite an ever growing tax burden, it has become impossible to pay for all the demands of the modern welfare state. At the same time, simply attempting to pay for those demands has slowed economic growth and left citizens poorer. A vicious circle was created, leaving countries unprepared to react to the onset of the financial crisis and the worldwide recession that followed.*

This book presents plenty of evidence that Tanner's observation is astutely correct.

In fact, Tanner's point is obvious enough that one cannot help but ask how Europe's political leaders, highly ranked economists and other public policy scholars failed to see the architecture of a looming structural crisis before it happened. Here, again, the explanation can be found in a strong, culturally cemented belief in automatic economic and social progress, as well as the irrefutable rationality of government and the welfare state.

---

4   Tanner, M., "Introduction: Europe's crisis and the welfare state," *Cato Journal*, Spring 2013. Available at: http://www.cato.org/sites/cato.org/files/serials/files/cato-journal/2013/5/cj33n2-intro.pdf, accessed December 27, 2013.

Europe's crisis sends a clear message, both to the United States and to other industrialized economies with big welfare states. It is a message of a deep, structural crisis that is immune to traditional economic policies. It is a crisis that calls for new measures to save prosperity—and for the fearless questioning of old truths.

Fragile Europe

If Europe maintains its conventional-wisdom slumber, the continent will pay a high price. Part of it is the descent into industrial poverty, a descent that is well exemplified by Greece. Not only has the country lost one quarter of its GDP, but it has now also been downgraded by three financial rating institutions from a developed market to an emerging market.[5] This unprecedented event effectively re-classifies Greece from a member of the advanced, industrialized world to a second-tier economy with permanently higher risks for global investors.

This downgrade will make it harder for Greece to attract foreign direct investment and thus make it costlier for the country to maintain whatever levels of prosperity it will have when the crisis stabilizes. It is yet another indication of the long-term transformation that is eclipsing more and more of Europe.

Another part of Europe's price for neglecting the true nature of its crisis has to do with disturbing changes on the political scene. Radical non-mainstream political parties are advancing their positions and in some cases threatening the status quo maintained by social democrats and liberals. Best known among them are the nationalist Front National in France, the socialist Syriza in Greece and the openly national-socialist Golden Dawn, also in Greece. Notably, in Portugal the Socialist Party, formed by militants in 1973, is the second largest with 32 percent of the seats in the national legislature.

The new wave of radicals, regardless of their political label, plays a more than marginal role in today's European politics. Their strong and growing support is telling of the severity of the crisis. The threat of an overall radicalization of European politics has risen to such prominence that renowned analysts have begun voicing their concerns. A good example is George Friedman, founder of global intelligence research firm Stratfor. On March 5, 2013, he explained

---

5 "Greece the economic wasteland," The Liberty Bullhorn, October 31, 2013. Available at: http://libertybullhorn.com/2013/10/31/greece-the-economic-wasteland/, accessed December 27, 2013.

that there is a link between high and lasting unemployment and political extremism:[6]

> Last week Italy held elections, and the party that won the most votes – with about a quarter of the total – was a brand-new group called the Five Star Movement that is led by a professional comedian. Two things are of interest about this movement. First, one of its central pillars is the call for defaulting on a part of Italy's debt as the lesser of evils. The second is that Italy, with 11.2 percent unemployment, is far from the worst case of unemployment in the European Union. Nevertheless, Italy is breeding radical parties deeply opposed to the austerity policies currently in place.

He also sees a connection between austerity and the crisis:

> One of the consequences of austerity is recession. The economies of many European countries, especially those in the eurozone, are now contracting, since austerity obviously means that less money will be available to purchase goods and services. If the primary goal is to stabilize the financial system, it makes sense. But whether financial stability can remain the primary goal depends on a consensus involving broad sectors of society. When unemployment emerges, that consensus shifts and the focus shifts with it. When unemployment becomes intense, then the entire political system can shift.

When employed against today's structural crisis, Europe's austerity measures not only fall flat to the ground, but in fact have entirely negative consequences. The economic crisis deepens, unemployment continues to rise, and austerity continues to erode the welfare state that large segments of Europe's population depend on. It is under such circumstances expectable that radical political movements, offering radical solutions, will gain in popularity.

When this radicalization trend is added to the tendency among mainstream political leaders to double down rather than to adapt to changing circumstances, the conditions are ripe for an unstable continuation of the current crisis. The stronger radical movements become, the graver the threat will be to the remaining prosperity, even to democracy, in Europe.

---

6   Friedman, G., "Europe, unemployment and instability," Stratfor Global Intelligence, March 5, 2013. Available at: http://www.stratfor.com/weekly/europe-unemployment-and-instability, accessed December 27, 2013.

George Friedman points to Italy as a good example. The recent election was more of an accelerator than a brake pedal in the ongoing crisis:

> *Portugal, Spain and Greece are in a depression. Their unemployment rate is roughly that of the United States in the midst of the Great Depression. A rule I use is that for each person unemployed, three others are affected, whether spouses, children or whomever. That means that when you hit 25 percent unemployment virtually everyone is affected. At 11 percent unemployment about 44 percent are affected … in Greece, for example, pharmaceuticals are now in short supply since cash for importing goods has dried up. Spain's local governments are about to lay off more employees. These countries have reached a tipping point from which it is difficult to imagine recovering. In the rest of Europe's periphery, the unemployment crisis is intensifying.*

Of particular worry is the situation in Greece, where neo-Nazi Golden Dawn was among the political winners in the 2012 elections.[7] Friedman sees potentially very serious consequences of this:

> *Fascism had its roots in Europe in massive economic failures in which the financial elites failed to recognize the political consequences of unemployment. They laughed at parties led by men who had been vagabonds selling post cards on the street and promising economic miracles if only those responsible for the misery of the country were purged. Men and women, plunged from the comfortable life of the petite bourgeoisie, did not laugh, but responded eagerly to that hope. The result was governments who enclosed their economies from the world and managed their performance through directive and manipulation … Whether it is the Golden Dawn party in Greece or the Catalan independence movements, the growth of parties wanting to redefine the system that has tilted so far against the middle class is inevitable.*

There are other political movements to factor in here, such as Jobbik and Fidesz in Hungary, the Front National in France, the new British nationalist coalition formed out of radical fringe parties, and a host of nationalist, even neo-Nazi, parties gaining ground in troubled Sweden. Nevertheless, Greece is a good test case for what this serious economic crisis can do to a country.

---

7 "Greek fascists winners in welfare state crisis," The Liberty Bullhorn, May 2, 2012. Available at: http://libertybullhorn.com/2012/05/02/greek-fascists-winners-in-welfare-state-crisis/, accessed December 27, 2013.

The symbolism in the June 2012 electoral success for Golden Dawn cannot be overstated: for the first time in 80 years, and right in the middle of a depression-style economic crisis, voters elect a Nazi party to a parliament in a European country.

This happened at the same time as the economic crisis spread like a bonfire from country to country. The crisis was followed by desperate slash-and-burn austerity policies, depression-level unemployment and widespread economic desperation.

Greece took an involuntary leadership role, demonstrating how an economic crisis can give momentum to political extremism. In addition to Golden Dawn, Greek voters also gave strong support to equally radical Syriza. This radical socialist party, which came in second in the election, has close ideological ties to Venezuela's deceased authoritarian president Hugo Chavez.

There were other extremist parties, among them traditional Soviet-style communists. A whopping 39 percent of the voters in Greece supported any one of the anti-democratic parties.

It deserves to be pointed out that despite the high unemployment and its relation to political extremism that George Friedman outlines, the average European voter has not yet given up on parliamentary democracy. The problem is that most of Europe's leaders still appear to believe that austerity is the only remedy for the crisis.[8] Thereby they are ready to perpetuate the very cause of their own economic hardship.

But the long-term trend is that support for parliamentary democracy is wearing thin. As governments continue to apply economic policies that exacerbate the crisis, more people will be driven into the arms of extremist parties.

Again, the test balloon will be Greece. With one quarter of its GDP gone; with unemployment closing in on 30 percent and youth unemployment at twice that level, the pressing question of the day is how long the Greek economy can last without collapsing. A related question is how much longer Greek voters

---

8   "Europeans still back austerity," CNN Money, May 13, 2013. Available at: http://money.cnn.com/2013/05/13/news/economy/europe-austerity-pew/index.html, accessed December 27, 2013.

are going to respect parliamentary democracy, a system that according to increasingly appealing Nazis and Chavista socialists bears some of the blame for the crisis.

And most important of all: if the economic crisis would drive Greece into the arms of either extremist faction, how much of a precedent would that set for extremists in other, equally badly hurt countries?

The force of this economic crisis is so strong that it threatens not just the prosperity and economic opportunity of future European generations, but also jeopardizes the broader institution of European society. This has not happened during any economic downturn this side of World War II. While the unraveling of parliamentary democracy is still highly unlikely, it can no longer be ruled out. As the crisis deepens, incumbent elected officials will be increasingly blamed for, and tied to, the economic wasteland opening up in the footsteps of the crisis. Since the vast majority of the so-called established parties in EU's troubled member states back the austerity policies that make life tough for people, there is a growing risk that voters increasingly will turn to alternatives to traditional representative democracy.

Crisis Unfolding

The role of government debt in the crisis has been under-reported. Yet its role in upsetting bank balance sheets is significant. It is an unprecedented phenomenon in our modern, advanced economies.

Government debt had been on the rise in most European countries in the years leading up to the crisis. Private-sector activity was slowing down and unemployment numbers, especially among the young, were trending upward. However, despite the tepid performance of Europe's economies in the years leading up to the current crisis, government bonds were still considered good investments.

It did not take long, though, after the crisis erupted before country after country in Europe reached unsustainable debt levels, putting their credit rating in jeopardy as a direct consequence. When Greece started having problems paying its creditors and other countries drifted into the same stormy waters, banks realized the low-risk end of their portfolios was evaporating.

The more heavily invested in Treasury bonds the banks were, the deeper they sank. The deeper they sank, the more radical were the consequences. A stunning example is the government-enforced confiscation of bank deposits in Cyprus in the spring of 2013. But the problems for Europe's financial institutions began long before that. Already in 2011 it was clear that Greece would write down its debt, effectively depriving lenders—banks included— of a significant amount of money. (The writedown eventually landed at 20 percent.) This did a fair amount of harm to the financial institutions involved. Since banks in Cyprus were heavily exposed to Greek Treasury bonds, they took major losses when the Greek government and the EU effectively forced them and other banks holding Greek bonds to accept the writedown.

The Greek debt writedown and the so-called Cypriot Bank Heist exemplify how the welfare state crisis fueled the bank crisis. But the crisis has also worked the other way, with governments providing bailouts to troubled banks. Together, the welfare-state crisis and the bank crisis have accelerated out of control, creating an unprecedented structural economic challenge to Europe's political leaders. Part of this challenge is to untangle the welfare state from the financial system—in plain English, to get government borrowing under control.

That is easier said than done. From 2007 when the European economy was still far away from the Great Recession, and 2011 when the crisis was in full bloom, the member states of the European Union sold one trillion euros worth of Treasury bonds to banks. The debt-to-GDP ratio for the EU rose from 62 percent in 2007 to 89 percent four years later. (Preliminary numbers put that rate at 95 percent for 2012.)

But Europe's welfare states have not just borrowed during the current economic crisis: they frivolously increased their debt in the good-times years before the current crisis. In 2003 the EU member states had a debt-to-GDP ratio of 59 percent, again up to 62 percent in 2007. In 2008, the year when the crisis began, the ratio was 66 percent.

This trend is disturbing enough to raise red flags at the EU level. But the warning signs were even bigger at the state level:

- Ireland had a stable debt-to-GDP ratio between 26 and 29 percent from 2003 to 2007, only to see it jump to 45 percent in 2008 (preliminary 2012 figure: 113 percent);

- Greece went from 93 percent in 2003 to 125 percent in 2008 (180 percent in 2012);

- The French debt ratio went from 61 percent of GDP in 2003 to 73 percent in 2008 (102 percent in 2012);

- Italy's debt ratio crept up every year, from 100 percent in 2003 to 113 percent in 2008 (143 percent in 2012);

- the Netherlands had a stable ratio averaging 49 percent through 2007, but experienced a sharp rise to 62 percent in 2008 (78 percent in 2012);

- Portugal's debt ratio went from 56 to 77 percent from 2003 to 2008 (135 percent in 2012).

From 2003 to 2008, GDP growth in Europe was relatively stable but not very strong. Unemployment was down after the Millennium Recession but not to the low levels seen in earlier decades.

The fact that several EU member states saw rising debt-to-GDP ratios during this period is a clear indication that there was an underlying structural problem in their economies. A sustainable welfare state should not force governments to rack up debt when the economy is doing relatively well. Yet that is precisely what happened between the Millennium and Great Recessions.

The message in these growing debt ratio numbers is that Europe's welfare states had reached a point where they were permanently unable to pay their bills. When the recession began in 2008 and accelerated in 2009, some welfare states rapidly reached a point where debt default could no longer be ruled out.

Greek and Spanish Treasury bonds turned so bad their governments had to pay more than 7 percent interest to move them.[9] In Spain, the decline of the country's government bonds closely coincided with a meltdown on the real estate market. This point was made clearly in the spring of 2013 by Professor Pedro Schwartz of the CEU San Pablo University in Madrid:[10]

---

9   Please see: http://www.tradingeconomics.com/spain/government-bond-yield and http://www.tradingeconomics.com/greece/government-bond-yield, accessed January 2014.

10   Lemieux, P., "American and European welfare states: similar causes, similar effects," *Cato Journal*, Spring 2013. Available at: http://www.cato.org/sites/cato.org/files/serials/files/cato-journal/2013/5/cj33n2-3.pdf, accessed December 27, 2013.

> *A housing bubble expanded by artificially depressed interest rates burst when the return on overvalued assets became too low to attract new investors. As the Spanish government, lacking the power to print money, moved to act as lender-of-last-resort to the financial sector, it discovered that it did not have the funds and could not borrow them, because it was incapacitated by a financial bubble of its own—an uncontrolled entitlement policy. A doubly severe sovereign debt crisis hit the economy.*

Adding even more insult to the injury, the European Union then started putting fiscal pressure on the countries at the crisis forefront: Greece, Spain, Portugal and Italy. Believing that they were dealing with a regular recession, the EU, together with the European Central Bank and the International Monetary Fund, demanded harsh austerity policies to rapidly close budget deficits. The theory was that higher taxes and spending cuts would eliminate the need for those states to borrow money, and perhaps even allow them to start paying down their debt. That in turn would lower interest rates which would encourage private businesses to start investing and get the economy out of the recession.

Or so the theory said. Reality proved to be a different animal. Already before austerity, and before the recession, Europe's economies had stagnated. There were signs of serious, long-term macroeconomic problems years before the Great Recession began. But it was not until the EU–ECB–IMF troika forced troubled states into austerity that theory and reality clashed.

At that moment, Europe's journey into industrial poverty gained serious momentum.

The current European version of austerity means that government takes more and more from taxpayers and gives less and less back. The exact combination of higher taxes and spending cuts defines the eventual outcome, but as applied in Europe during the current crisis austerity has meant a destructive combination of both. By means of higher taxes, government has taken more and taxpayers have less to spend, yet at the same time government has cut spending, giving less back to the economy. Inevitably, this results in a net loss of spending in the economy.

As a result of higher taxes and lower spending, GDP growth slows down. This in turn leads to stagnant incomes, contributing to the long-term stagnation in standard of living.

As the economic wheels grind to a halt, the gates are opened to industrial poverty. Once an economy gets stuck there, it will remain there for as long as policy-makers focus more of their efforts on preserving the welfare state than on reforming it.

Europe's young are among the millions of Europeans paying the price for economic stagnation. In 2013 youth unemployment rates in the EU reached the 20-20 level: in 20 EU member states, youth unemployment was 20 percent or higher.

There is no end in sight. Every year, a new class leaves school, with one in five in most EU member states being offered unemployment as a career opener. An entire generation of young Europeans could end up with a life-long net debt to government: they could in the aggregate end up consuming more of government services and entitlements than they pay for through taxes.

There is a terrible price to pay in this for tens of millions of young people. They get off to a bad start early on in life and cannot get a foot in the door of the labor market. They are, in a sense, truncated both socially and economically. As prospective life-long consumers of the welfare state they can never experience the pride that lies in determining one's own path in life.

As if this was not enough, the prospect of an entire generation of net government consumers opens a vicious economic circle. When each new generation that enters adulthood becomes a net cost to the welfare state, government finds it increasingly difficult to balance its budget. This is true even if most young people get a job: when GDP grows very slowly, as it has in Europe for the better part of two decades now, people's incomes grow slowly. This leads to slow growth in tax revenues, while more people remain dependent on the welfare state—even those who are working.

When tax revenues rise more slowly than what the welfare state needs for its entitlement programs, the budget deficit becomes permanent. The gut reaction from Europe's political leaders will in all likelihood be more of the same.

More austerity.

What is Industrial Poverty?

The next question is: what is Europe going to be when this crisis is over? The answer to this question is the second step of the hypothesis of industrial poverty. It has two parts to it: one narrative, one quantitative. Let us begin with the former.

Life under industrial poverty is static. Tomorrow offers nothing better than yesterday. People still have access to the basic conveniences of an industrialized society, but there is no change for the better in the quality of life.

People don't have to chop wood to heat their homes; they don't have to ride horseback but can use motorized transportation; they have a health care system that can treat basic medical conditions; there are schools that provide all children with basic life skills. But nothing ever gets better. The car that your grandchild will buy will essentially be the same as the car your grandfather drove.

If there is any change, it is in the form of a slow but inevitable decline. This decline is particularly obvious in health care. Rationing slowly nibbles away at more and more health care services. Waiting times to see the doctor continue to grow, and just to avoid them people have to pay higher taxes, or higher fees at the clinic (or both). The government monopoly on health care makes more and more health services inaccessible, either through fees or through rationing.

Other sectors also suffer: schools slowly deteriorate; tax-funded retirement systems pay less and less per dollar earned while working.

At best, households experience static purchasing power, but they are just as likely to see the value of their paychecks slowly decline. Because of the slow nature of the process, it takes a while before it becomes obvious in economic data. But the citizens feel the squeeze in their lives, where the same amount of work that previously led to progress in their standard of living now at best barely keeps them afloat.

This is not a purely theoretical construct. While Europe still has not reached a state that we could definitely classify as industrial poverty, there are individual examples to illustrate the concept. In the 1990s industrial poverty came roaring into Sweden with lots of fanfare. Over the past five years Greece has had a similar experience. There are also examples of slower yet no doubt agonizing stagnation and decline, such as in Spain or Italy over the past decade.

The Portuguese economy is almost to the euro of the same size today as it was 10 years ago.

Industrial poverty is hard to identify with the traditional economic measurements, but there are a few indicators that can help us put numbers on it:

- stagnation in private consumption;

- the decline in private consumption as an important economic variable;

- high youth unemployment; and

- oversized government (not to be confused with the vague term "big government").

These four variables are relatively easy to test, and we shall do so later on. A country that scores "bad" enough on all these four indicators is a country that is either in, or on the verge of, industrial poverty.

There is, however, another symptom of industrial poverty that deserves attention. It has to do with why we work. In a strong-growing, well-working economy we get a job and build a career in order to become more prosperous. We educate ourselves, work our way up or start businesses in good part because we want to grow our personal finances and make life better for our family. As a result, we prosper.[11]

In economies that are close to the danger zone of stagnation, such as economies with a government near the oversize limit, people work for a different motive, namely to keep up with cost of living. One part of their cost of living is government, primarily in the form of high taxes. This is not just a rhetorical point used by conservatives or libertarians: the transition from *working for ourselves* to *living off government* to *working for government* is statistically visible. The relation between workforce participation and taxes as share of GDP is in fact U-shaped. We can illustrate this with two U.S. states and a European country with an elaborate welfare state:

---

11 Larson, S.R., "The economic case for limited government," *Prosperitas* Vol. VII, Issue III, April 2007, Center for Freedom and Prosperity. Available at: http://archive.freedomandprosperity. org/Papers/rahncurve/rahncurve.pdf, accessed December 27, 2013.

- in a low-tax jurisdiction, such as the U.S. state of Wyoming with a 7.3 percent tax-to-GDP ratio, workforce participation is at 75.8 percent (both from 2007);

- in New York, taxes are 11.9 percent of GDP and workforce participation is a lowly 67.8 percent (both from 2007).

It is important to point out that the tax-to-GDP ratios for these two states do not include the tax burden imposed by the federal government, as that burden is the same for all states. The important point is that within a certain spectrum there is a negative correlation between the tax burden and workforce participation.

Outside that spectrum, though, the relation is reversed (see Figure 1.1).

As government grows beyond its "New York" size, both government spending and taxes go up. To answer that question we need to look at European countries. In 2007 Sweden and Denmark had the highest tax-to-GDP ratios in the European Union (48.3 and 48.7 percent, respectively). They also had among the highest workforce participation ratios (74.2 and 77.1 percent, respectively).

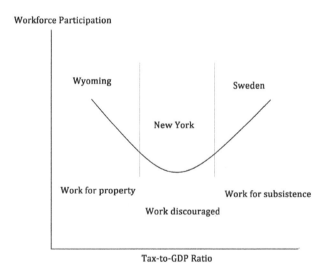

Figure 1.1   Workforce participation and taxes
Sources: U.S. Bureau of Economic Analysis, U.S. Bureau of Labor Statistics, OECD and Eurostat.

While the U.S. states generally line up on the downslope from "Wyoming" to "New York," the more heavily taxed states in the EU generally line up along the upslope from "New York" to "Sweden."

As the welfare state expands, its taxes discourage work (its entitlement programs do the same). People work less than they did when they worked predominantly for themselves. They earn less, of course, but the welfare state compensates people for their reduced workforce participation. This plays out as a shift in generational behavior: people who enter the workforce under the welfare state make different choices than those who entered the workforce a generation earlier.

So long as we are on the downward slope from "Wyoming" to "New York" there is no considerable risk for economic stagnation. As is evident from Europe over the past few years, that is something that gradually works its way into economies on the right-hand upslope. Eventually, government becomes too big for households to pay for—they work "for the welfare state" instead of their own finances—and we reach the point of economic stagnation.

The transition from "Wyoming" to "Sweden" can happen to any industrialized country. The United States is not immune to the mechanisms that have trapped Europe in economic stagnation. If the United States so decided, it could fight its budget deficit the same way as the Europeans have; over time, economic activity would decline and bring the U.S. economy into compliance with the four aforementioned indicators of industrial poverty:

- stagnation in private consumption;

- the decline in private consumption as an important economic variable;

- high youth unemployment; and

- oversized government.

Government does not have to be "big" in itself, only too big for the private sector to pay for. In other words, the oversize measurement is a ratio with government spending in the numerator and GDP in the denominator. This means that government can drift into industrial poverty either of two ways: by excessive expansion of spending or by experiencing a sustained stagnation in GDP.

In some cases, both of these things happen at the same time. Chapter 2 offers an example, namely the Swedish economic crisis in the 1990s. This crisis shares some key elements with the current situation in Europe both in terms of the nature of the crisis and when it comes to the policies used in a botched attempt at restoring the economy pre-crisis levels.

After the Swedish chapter we will develop a detailed understanding for how to quantitatively test whether or not an economy is in industrial poverty. We will apply this test to Sweden, then proceed to apply it to the current crisis in Europe.

Chapter 2
Sweden: Austerity Gone Wrong

On Friday, September 18, 1992, I was at a bar on the campus of the University of Stockholm. I was hanging out with a bunch of other politics junkies, having conversations about everything from the latest meeting with the student assembly to the political and economic turmoil that was plaguing Europe in the summer and early fall of 1992.

It was the last workday before the French referendum on the new European Union constitution, known at the time as the Maastricht Treaty. All self-proclaimed political experts in the bar, me included, did our best to predict which way the French were going to vote. We really had no way of predicting, but we knew one thing for certain: if the French voted no it would be the end of the attempts to form the brave, new European Union.

Halfway through the night my friend Alfred showed up. He was one of the lucky few who had gotten an internship with the new, center-right government under Mr. Carl Bildt. Young and ambitious as he was, Alfred had been given the opportunity to work directly under treasury secretary Anne Wibble.

He stopped by the bar on the university campus to see friends and brag about his prestigious internship. As we flocked around him, he shared generic gossip and dropped names like quarters in a wishing pond.

Alfred was smart, though. He knew that there were some things he could not talk about. If he did, it would quickly get back to his bosses. Sweden is a small country, and the circles of politicians and political wannabes are even smaller. Everyone knows everyone's friends.

As Alfred shared his generic anecdotes, most of his audience got bored. They wanted to hear more juicy stories, but he was not going to give them more. They left.

I, too, wanted to hear more, but not gossip. I wanted to know what people in Prime Minister Bildt's cabinet thought about the economic and political turbulence in Europe at that time. Sweden was right in the middle of a deep economic crisis, part of which was related to a broader crisis in Europe. Speculation about the future of the new EU constitution spilled over into Sweden, putting the Swedish central bank under heavy pressure from global currency speculators.

Most speculators believed that the central bank would not be able to keep its fixed exchange rate much longer.

The question was: when would the Swedish krona fall?

Whoever was the first to know would make a lot of money. And whoever knew but was not allowed to talk about it, would be well advised not to spill the beans.

Alfred knew, and he was not supposed to talk about it. But he did. Halfway into his third beer for the night, he took a step closer to me, leaned over and said in a hushed voice that "if France votes no to Maastricht" the central bank would devalue the currency on the following Monday, September 21. In other words, if the French people rejected the proposed constitution for the European Union in a referendum on September 20, the Swedish central bank would cave in to international currency speculators.

With those words my friend disappeared into the intoxicated crowd, leaving me with one of the most valuable pieces of information I had ever had. As it turned out, the French eventually voted yes to the Maastricht Treaty, though with the smallest of margins. The Swedish fixed exchange rate survived, but not for long. After having tried to fend off the global currency speculators with a financial ice-age style 500 percent interest rate the Swedish Central Bank gave up in November of 1992. The krona depreciated quickly and violently.

By that time the turbulence in the rest of Europe had subsided. One of the toughest years in recent history for the European economy was coming to an end. Sweden was hit particularly hard, struggling with the worst economic crisis since the Great Depression:[1]

- 15 percent of the workforce lost their jobs in 18 months;

---

1   Statistics Sweden, please see www.scb.se, accessed December 27, 2013.

- inflation touched double digits for two years;

- a new tax system had raised taxes sharply on consumer spending;

- GDP was shrinking for the third year in a row; and

- government was running a budget deficit in excess of 10 percent of GDP.

The tax reform caused a depression of consumer spending in the years leading up to the 1992 crisis. Businesses, large and small, were more concerned with shutting down operations than investing for the future. Government was panicking over the overwhelming costs for welfare and unemployment benefits caused by the depression-style recession. And economists and analysts were staring in disbelief at the runaway budget deficit.

To some degree, today's Greece is exhibiting the same macroeconomic symptoms as Sweden did in 1992. It has a large, persistent budget deficit, shrinking GDP, mass unemployment and an economics profession that is strikingly perplexed by the crisis. Therefore, the Swedish crisis furnishes us with an important learning opportunity as we try to understand why Greece — and other European welfare states — are stuck in a deep crisis.

Sweden's prime minister in 1992, Mr. Carl Bildt, and his governing center-right coalition did not address the deficit directly. They did not try to encourage more private spending, but they also refrained from austerity. Their choice was instead a norm-based fiscal policy strategy designed by treasury secretary Anne Wibble. The idea was to create a set of long-term economic-policy rules that would form a predictable framework for the private sector. This norm-based strategy meant that government would take a hands-off approach to short-term problems, let the private sector grow and thereby get the economy going again. As for the budget deficit the idea was that it would start shrinking once the private sector felt confident enough to invest and hire more people.

There was some logic to the choice of a norm-based strategy. During the turbulent economic decline in 1990–91 the private sector had seen its confidence in the future be shattered by high inflation, a radical tax reform that few knew the effects of, a sharp downturn in the global economy and a major crisis in the Swedish banking system. The Bildt administration's norm-based policies provided a little bit of a safe haven, especially during the turbulence of 1992.

That said, norm-based policy can only work indirectly to restore economic growth and full employment. If businesses are faced with a depressed market for their products, with no credible chance of improvement, they will not invest or hire more people regardless of how steadfastly government commits to long-term predictability.

This was exactly the situation in Sweden in 1992. The Bildt administration desperately needed growth in private-sector activity to restore full employment and eradicate the budget deficit. But none of that happened. Export-oriented businesses were faced with tough competition in tight markets, and before the krona fell in November of 1992 they were at a currency disadvantage. Firms that sold on the domestic market faced a shrinking GDP, depressed household expectations and an unemployment rate that severely restricted consumer spending.

Since norm-based policies do not have any immediate effects on the budget deficit, and since the economy overall was in a depressed state, there were serious questions in 1992 how long Sweden would be able to sustain a budget deficit at 10 percent of GDP. As a result of the deep economic crisis, the depressed private sector and the vast welfare-state entitlement systems, government spending was at 60 percent of GDP.[2]

Between the fixed exchange rate and the norm-based fiscal policy, nothing was moving that could reduce the budget deficit. Something had to give. Either treasury secretary Wibble would have to become more interventionist, or the central bank would have to give up its defense of the fixed exchange rate.

The rumor I heard about a devaluation of the currency in September indicated that the central bank would probably be the first one to surrender. Two months later, it did. In a short period of time the Swedish krona lost enormously in value, plunging initially from 5 krona per U.S. dollar to 8 krona per U.S. dollar.

While this depreciation led to a rapid rise in prices on imports, it also became a bit of a blessing for the Swedish economy. Sweden's large manufacturing corporations, traditionally important to the economy, could suddenly cut their prices on foreign markets. They could cut prices essentially overnight on all sorts of exports: cars, heavy trucks, industrial tools, power plant components,

---

2   Statistics Sweden, www.scb.se, accessed December 27, 2013. See also Eurostat government finance statistics, available at: http://epp.eurostat.ec.europa.eu/portal/page/portal/government_finance_statistics/introduction, accessed December 27, 2013.

cell phones, mine drilling equipment, chainsaws, paper pulp, mass transit buses … and they made more money in the bargain.

Sweden experienced an exports rally in 1993 and 1994. As a result, the economy got back on something that looked like a recovery path. The steep decline in the employment rate flattened out and the gaping hole in the government budget was not growing out of control anymore. The stock market improved dramatically.

Was the end of the depression in sight? Had Sweden turned a corner? Would exports pull the economy back to full employment?

Again, we can see a parallel to today's Greece. Some critics of current Greek austerity policies have suggested that the country should leave the euro and reintroduce its own currency, the drachma. That currency shift would almost certainly constitute a de facto devaluation of the Greek currency, prompting the same questions as we asked about Sweden in 1992: would it be the beginning of the end of the Greek recession? Would it mean that Greece could turn a corner? Would the following rise in exports pull the Greek economy back to full employment?

Before we speculate as to what the answer might be to these questions, let us establish that the answers to these questions about Sweden are, respectively: no, there was no end to the depression in sight; maybe Sweden had turned a corner; and no, exports alone cannot pull a welfare state out of a recession.

All that a strong upswing in exports can do is provide lawmakers with a window of opportunity, a little bit of fiscal-policy breathing space, but not more. A stabilized unemployment rate and a budget deficit that is no longer running away from home give a savvy government the window of opportunity to put the economy back on track again.

In 1993 and 1994 the Bildt administration had this window of opportunity. The budget deficit decreased by a notable 13.4 percent in 1994 and the public sentiment of economic panic was gone. Nobody could seriously believe that the economy was en route to normal, but the sense of catch-your-breath temporary stability offered a golden moment for the government to do something to further encourage private-sector growth. As part of such a strategy the Bildt administration could have addressed the structural imbalance imposed upon the economy by the costly welfare state. They could have:

- executed a clearly defined, predictable package of spending cuts to align government services with the conditions under which private businesses operate; this would have guaranteed lower long-term costs to taxpayers and opened for privatization;

- deregulated markets under government monopoly to allow private competitors; this would have been especially welcome in health care and health insurance;

- initiated privatization of the country's costly government-run income insurance programs.

Combined with steadfast norms to vouch for a predictable tax and regulatory environment for businesses, these reforms would have helped the economy grow faster, create more jobs and still reduce the budget deficit. One way this would be accomplished is through the opening of new sectors of the economy to private entrepreneurship and lots of new jobs.

Yet the Bildt administration did nothing. It failed to seize the macroeconomic moment and, even more importantly, in the campaign leading up to the September 1994 election it failed to explain to voters why its policies were preferable to the alternative that the social democrats put forward.

From Norms to Austerity

Having governed Sweden uninterruptedly for 44 years, from 1932 to 1976, the social democrats earned a global reputation for creating a welfare state like no other. It redistributed income and resources between citizens on a scale not seen west of the Berlin Wall, supposedly without doing the same harm to the private sector that a full-blown communist system does.

When the 1970s came around, signs of structural ailment in the private sector began to emerge. GDP growth slowed, partly but not entirely because of the two oil crises in 1973 and 1979. In the early 1970s taxes exceeded the critical 40 percent threshold beyond which the private sector is no longer able to adapt and cope under the pressure from government. Private consumption stagnated, as did tax revenues.

Already then, Sweden was confronted with some of the characteristics of industrial poverty. However, it managed to fend off the inevitable, permanent crisis that comes with industrial poverty. Instead the country limped through the 1980s thanks in part to several aggressive currency devaluations in the late 1970s and early 1980s. A deregulation of the financial sector contributed to some degree, but there was only a modest growth in consumer spending. Instead, the banks focused on lending to real estate and stock-market speculation.

The only ones that did very well in the 1980s were the export-oriented big corporations. By the end of the 1980s the exports boom tapered off as a remarkable growth period in global trade came to a halt. In 1990 there were serious signs of a recession. Its causes were to be found in a combination of a weakening international economy, a sluggish domestic sector unable to compensate for dropping exports, and a tax reform in 1990 that discouraged consumer spending just as total demand in the economy was in decline.

A real estate crash in 1990 aggravated the crisis. The social democrats, who had regained power in 1982, were blamed for the tumbling economy and lost the election in 1991.

By 1994 they were ripe and ready to return to power, and focused their election campaign on the need for action against the budget deficit. Where Prime Minister Bildt wanted long-term norms to do the magic trick, the social-democrat candidate for prime minister, Mr. Carlsson, successfully portrayed Mr. Bildt as passive, inept and clueless when it came to the deficit.

As his alternative, Mr. Carlsson suggested that a balanced budget was the first line of defense of the welfare state.

The strategy worked. In September of 1994 a majority of voters decided that it was time to put the social democrats back in the driver's seat. Having been promised a prudent fiscal-policy approach to budget cuts they apparently bought the notion that the welfare state was not only salvageable but that the center-right coalition was unable to do so.

Once in power, the social democrats offered nothing that could be defined as "prudent," especially not on the fiscal-policy front.

Six weeks after their electoral victory, in November of 1994, they introduced a bill to the national parliament, the Riksdag, with the inconspicuous title "Certain economic-policy measures, etc." In this bill, which was not a formal budget bill but more of a declaration of intent, Prime Minister Carlsson and his treasury secretary Mr. Persson explained their ambition to eradicate the budget deficit. The bill was a big austerity package, and the administration did not mince their words:[3]

> The purpose of [the administration's] economic policy is now to cleanse the budget of its deficit in order to attain sustainable, enduring growth, increased employment and decreased unemployment. After a period of sharply declining production and increasing unemployment, the economic policy is now focused on increasing employment and creating conditions for high general welfare by means of low unemployment, price stability and strong economic growth. A necessary starting point for this [policy strategy] is to stabilize the ratio of government debt to GDP no later than in 1998.

There is an important policy declaration in this paragraph that has to do with the statement about deficit "cleansing." This word is a literal translation from Swedish, intentionally conveying the sentiment toward the deficit in the austerity plan. Unlike its predecessor the Carlsson administration made reducing and eventually eliminating the budget deficit its top fiscal-policy priority. Where the Bildt administration had sought to create a long-term stable environment for the private sector, hoping to inspire economic growth and a reduction in unemployment, the Carlsson administration ranked any other policy goal second to balancing the budget.

Technically, the austerity plan links the budget balancing goal to "sustainable growth, increased employment and decreased unemployment." (As we will see in a coming chapter, this is not unlike the rhetoric used by the European Union in its imposing austerity on Greece and other EU member states.) However, the outcomes of the policy do not provide any support for a causal link from budget-balancing austerity to growth and full employment. During the entire three-year period when the austerity plan was being implemented the Swedish economy saw neither a recovery in "sustainable" growth nor a drop in unemployment. On the contrary, the employment rate among 16–64-year-olds actually fell from the start of the austerity policies in 1995 to their end in 1998.

Prevailing economic theory supports austerity if and only if:

---

3   *Regeringens proposition* 1994/95:25, available at: http://www.riksdagen.se/sv/Dokument-Lagar/ Forslag/Propositioner-och-skrivelser/prop-19949525-Vissa-ekonomis_GI0325/, accessed December 27, 2013.

1. government borrowing pushes interest rates up—a so-called crowding-out effect;

2. an elimination of government borrowing lowers interest rates; and

3. the private sector uses the lower interest rates to substantially expand spending (e.g., corporate investments).

The problem for the Swedish economy is that this causal chain of events did not happen. Contrary to what theory would suggest, the inflation-adjusted growth rate in private investments fell during the austerity policies. More specifically, in fixed prices Swedish manufacturers kept their investments flat during most of the austerity years, as well as a couple of years after they ended. Since the manufacturers were the ones that benefited the most from the exports boom following the 1992 currency collapse, it would have been logical if they were the ones to benefit from the austerity policies. The fact that they did not substantially expand their investments is clear evidence that the causal chain suggested by economic theory did not go to work in Sweden.

If the social-democrat administration had put other economic goals than a balanced government budget on par with that goal, it would have been easy for them to monitor key economic variables and gauge whether or not their policies were having the intended effects. Since they did not change their policies as employment and investments failed to respond, one cannot draw any other conclusion than that the balanced budget was *their only* policy goal.

This is consistent with the goal behind austerity policies in today's Greece, Spain, Portugal and Italy. There, governments have executed budget cuts and tax increases to balance their budgets in order to bring down interest rates. Especially the Greek example shows that no other economic-policy goals have been granted even comparable status; in their pursuit of a balanced budget, the Greek government has eradicated one quarter of the nation's GDP.

The Swedish government of 1995 did not eradicate any part of GDP. They did however permanently and substantially reduce the employment rate, an indicator that employment was of no consequence to them during the years of austerity.

In conclusion, alas, the first policy declaration of the social-democrat government's austerity plan was to replace a broad range of economic-policy goals with one and one only: to balance the government budget.

Another policy declaration in the austerity plan has to do with the reference to "general welfare." This term is a direct reference to the welfare state. The Carlsson administration set out to save the Swedish welfare state and to do so by means of a balanced budget. At the time there were widespread concerns, especially in the ranks of the social-democrat party, that an enduring budget deficit would eventually force the termination of the welfare state. This would happen as foreign creditors would become powerful enough to dictate the country's fiscal policy, and thus effectively neutralize parliamentary democracy.

In theory, there is some truth to this. Voters in the EU's currently most troubled welfare states, such as Greece and Italy, have seen first-hand how an out-of-control government deficit has led the EU to effectively terminate their parliamentary processes. Instead the EU–ECB–IMF troika de facto took charge of both the legislative and the executive branches of government.

In practice, though, the risk for such a foreign takeover was minimal, especially since the budget deficit peaked in 1993 and was in its second year of decline when the social democrats took office in late 1994.

Yet treasury secretary Persson was convinced that austerity was the only way forward. His proposal in the aforementioned strategic policy bill was to combine tax increases and spending cuts to a total value of 7 percent of GDP.[4]

Tax increases represented about 63 percent of the fiscal value of the austerity package, with increases in personal income taxes representing just over half of the total extra tax revenue. Almost one-fifth of the total amount came from a new top income-tax bracket.

Middle-class families who did not make enough to qualify for the new top bracket did not escape unscathed. They were hit by two tax increases, one clearly visible and one convoluted. The visible tax increase was an additional social security tax designed to fund the existing general income security system. The convoluted tax increase consisted of a slowed-down indexation of tax brackets. While technically not raising tax rates, this form of a tax increase forces taxpayers up into higher tax brackets even if their real earnings do not increase.

Increases in capital gains, property, dividend and retirement savings taxes, and a reinstatement of the wealth tax, accounted for 43 percent of the extra tax revenue that the Carlsson administration was hoping to get from the austerity

---

4   *Regeringens proposition* 1994/95:25, p. 9, Table 1.1.

package. A minor reduction in the corporate income tax probably did not make any difference for the better compared to the negative impact of the investment-oriented taxes.

The increase in the tax burden on households is clearly visible in economic statistics from the period. As a result of the higher level, Swedish families saw their disposable incomes decline. In 1996, right in the middle of the austerity package, they paid 104.58 kronas in more taxes for every 100 kronas they got in pay raise.

Another way to put this: according to Statistics Sweden (SCB), taxes as share of GDP rose from 60.1 percent of GDP in 1995 to 65.1 percent of GDP in 1998 (in current prices).[5]

Yet another angle is to divide the total amount of taxes paid in the Swedish economy by the number of people employed. (Since the working share of the population has to feed the non-working share, the tax burden per employed person gives us a good picture of the government-imposed support burden.) From 1994 to 1998 this ratio increased by 25.1 percent: if a Swedish taxpayer had to produce 1,000 kronas in taxes in 1994, he was responsible for 1,251 kronas in taxes four years later.

In addition to tax increases the austerity package also reduced entitlement spending. This kind of austerity measure is sometimes considered less harmful than tax increases. However, in a complex welfare state like the Swedish, cuts in entitlements have directly negative effects on consumer spending and thereby directly negative effects on overall economic activity. The combination of very high taxes and frivolous entitlements makes middle-class families dependent on government to make ends meet every month. A cut in entitlements without a corresponding, proportionate cut in taxes inevitably reduces their disposable income.

Entitlement cuts amounted to 37 percent of the fiscal value of the Swedish austerity package. There were five cuts that took direct aim at low- and middle-income families:

- a repeal of an entitlement aimed at supporting stay-at-home parents ("vårdnadsbidrag");

---

5   Statistics Sweden, National Accounts Statistics. Available at: www.scb.se, accessed December 27, 2013.

- weakened general income security;

- a repeal of an extra child benefit to families with many children ("flerbarnstillägg");

- a repeal of a form of alimony anticipation benefit ("bidragsförskott");

- a slowdown of indexation of retirement benefits and other income compensation benefits.

These cuts were designed to reduce the government's expenses for parts of what is generally referred to as "social protection spending," historically a large share of government spending in Sweden.

According to Eurostat standards, social protection spending includes the equivalent of the American OASDI plus compensation for lost income related to sickness, unemployment benefits, benefits to families with children, housing subsidies and so-called "social exclusion" entitlements. The last kind is typically a form of extra entitlement paid out to groups of citizens who are defined as "marginalized."

In 1995 Sweden led Europe in terms of social protection spending, with its sum total equal to 33.5 percent of GDP (see Table 2.1).

Table 2.1   European countries with social protection spending exceeding 25 percent of GDP

	1995
Sweden	**33.5**
Denmark	31.9
Finland	31.4
Netherlands	30.6
France	30.3
Austria	28.8
Germany	28.3
Belgium	27.3
United Kingdom	27.3
Norway	26.5

Source: Eurostat.

As a result of the austerity package, social protection spending as share of GDP declined (see Table 2.2).

Table 2.2   Workforce employment share, Sweden, age group 16–64

	2000
Sweden	**29.9**
Germany	29.7
France	29.5
Denmark	28.9
Austria	28.3
United Kingdom	26.4
Netherlands	26.4
Belgium	25.4
Finland	25.1

Source: Eurostat.

The decline in Swedish social protection spending coincides with a steep decline in the budget deficit. Based on this one could make the case that austerity worked against the deficit. However, as Figure 2.1 shows, the deficit decline began before the austerity policies began.

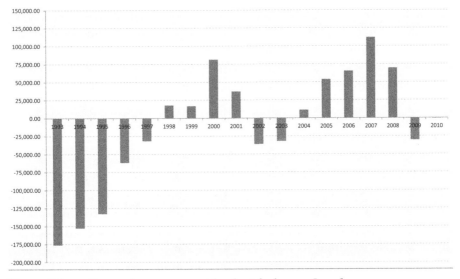

Figure 2.1   General government budget balance, Sweden
Source: Statistics Sweden, www.scb.se.

The austerity package was introduced to the Riksdag, the Swedish parliament, in November of 1994. Its policies went into effect during the latter half of 1995, which means that the decline in the budget deficit in 1996 and 1997 and eventual emergence of a surplus in 1998 are the results of this package. The decline in the budget deficit in 1994 and for the most part in 1995 cannot be attributed to austerity.

Does this mean we can draw the conclusion that austerity worked in Sweden, as opposed to Europe's southern countries?

The answer depends on the policy goal behind the austerity measures. In the Swedish case the goal was exclusively and solely to eliminate the budget deficit. The same goal lies behind today's European austerity efforts, leading to the conclusion that, yes, austerity worked in Sweden but has not worked in Greece, Spain, Portugal and other contemporary examples.

This, however, is a rather useless answer. First of all, the Swedish austerity program was implemented shortly after the currency depreciation, causing very rapid growth in exports. With that sector in rapid growth the Swedish government had some "macroeconomic padding" that today's Southern European countries do not have.

That said, Sweden paid a high price for its austerity years, with a permanent lowering of employment and a serious erosion of household finances. Therefore, it is valid to ask: could Sweden have used another kind of austerity, or even an entirely different fiscal policy approach, to achieve the same goal for the budget but without the steep macroeconomic price tag attached to it?

The answer to this question will have to wait until a later chapter.

Recalibrating the Welfare State

A valid question about the Swedish austerity experience is whether or not a different composition of austerity measures would have yielded a different result. While there was never any debate about the balance between tax hikes and spending cuts (at least not until after they had been implemented and the effects became apparent to welfare-state consumers) there is a rich research literature on this subject. A survey of this literature can help us understand whether or not Sweden in the 1990s, or Greece, Spain, Portugal, Italy, etc. today could have achieved a better macroeconomic outcome by choosing a different portfolio of austerity measures.

While it would be valid to discuss this here, such a discussion would by necessity be confined to the case of Sweden. Therefore, a later chapter will discuss the austerity literature and the potential success (or lack thereof) of other policy combinations.

One point, though, related to the composition issue, is that measures on the spending side of the government budget will always have direct effects on the design and operation of the welfare state. A cut in spending on, for example, unemployment benefits redefines the role of the welfare state, both immediately and over time. This redefinition affects economic behavior, especially when households have been led to rely on government for income security, and that income security is changed for the worse.

The Swedish austerity package redefined the welfare state by recalibrating its interaction with the rest of the economy. To understand what this means, let us begin with "translating" the policy measures to an American context. If Congress decided to match the Swedish austerity package for the fiscal year of 2014, it would have to raise taxes and cut entitlement spending by a total of $1.15 trillion. This number includes higher taxes on wealth, capital gains, dividends and IRA plans, plus the introduction of a federal property tax.

The part that would directly impact household income would be worth $260 billion.

It is not difficult to imagine the impact on the U.S. economy from an austerity package with $1.15 trillion in higher taxes and spending cuts. Even if it was phased in over three years, this large an austerity program would make a very big dent in the U.S. economy.

Interestingly, a package of this size has already been proposed. As part of his 2012 bid for the Republican presidential nomination, Congressman Ron Paul declared that he was willing to cut $1 trillion from the federal budget, and that he would be willing to do so within the first year of his presidency.[6] This would amount to approximately 27 percent of total federal spending.[7]

---

6   Please see the Congressman's presidential campaign website: http://www.ronpaul2012.com/ the-issues/ron-paul-plan-to-restore-america/, accessed April 7, 2013.

7   Please see: http://www.whitehouse.gov/sites/default/files/omb/budget/fy2012/assets/tables. pdf, accessed December 27, 2013.

Unlike the Swedish austerity plan the Ron Paul plan would concentrate entirely on spending cuts. Is this preferable to the mixed approach taken by the Swedish government? In the hypothetical U.S. case, that question is best answered by a quick review of what the actual spending cuts might look like.

Mandatory spending programs, primarily Social Security, Medicare, Medicaid, constitute $2.1 trillion of the budget. Assuming that Congress would never rally around deep cuts into these programs, we have to apply the $1 trillion in cuts to the remaining $1.6 trillion of the federal budget.

Even if we eliminated every single non-military, non-homeland security spending item, we could cut $395 billion. Adding to that the elimination of "overseas contingency operations" and miscellaneous irregular military/security programs we can total $692 billion in cuts.

All that remains of the federal government is now the Department of Defense and the Social Security–Medicare–Medicaid entitlement trio.

And we still have $308 billion to cut. If we distribute them evenly across the three entitlement programs we would reduce every Social Security check by 20 percent.

This translation of the Swedish austerity program to American terms tells us two things. First, it shows that it is difficult to drastically cut government spending in a short period of time without causing undue harm to people who have become critically dependent on government to make ends meet every week. There is no doubt that Congress must unite around a spending-cut plan, but such a plan cannot be based on the simplistic notion of massive, across-the-board cuts in a very short period of time. To bring lasting results, spending cuts require time, political courage and fiscal commitment over a long period of time. It is not only possible, but necessary, to reduce government spending, in Sweden in the 1990s as well as in the United States today—but in order to have a permanent effect on the budget the spending cuts must be done right.[8]

Second, the comparison between the U.S. federal budget and Sweden tells us just how big and complex the Swedish welfare state really is. At the time when the social-democrat government put its austerity plan to work, total

---

8   Larson, S.R., *Ending the Welfare State: A Path to Limited Government That Won't Leave the Poor Behind*, Outskirts Press, Denver, 2012.

government spending in Sweden reached 60 percent of GDP. That would be equivalent to $9.8 trillion in the United States in 2013.

At that spending level, government has become an intricate and very deeply rooted part of the economy. It nestles itself in to the private finances of most families, offering a host of entitlements and charging a plethora of taxes to pay for them.

A crucial part of the entitlement package is a general income security system. This system, basically unknown to Americans, is a way for government to socialize income protection, as government promises to replace people's income for a variety of specified reasons, such as:

- sick leave—instead of your employer giving you sick days, government replaces your salary up to a certain percentage;

- parental leave—when you have a child government replaces your salary for up to 12 months;

- caring for a sick child—government gives you the right to be home a certain number of days per year with a child that is too sick to go to school;

- caring for a sick relative—under some circumstances government pays your salary so you can care for an ailing, older relative.

The typical income replacement rate in these systems has been 75–80 percent, meaning that if you make $25 per hour government pays you up to $20 per hour for the days you are home sick or home with a newborn baby.

These programs are paid for with a payroll tax that, including taxes for the retirement system, are twice as high as they are in the United States. The payouts from the non-retirement income security systems equal, on average, 10 percent of the disposable income of Sweden's households, but they are far more important for low- and middle-income families than this number indicates.

Here we have a first key to what price Swedish households paid for the austerity package. The combined effect of the package on household disposable income amounted to 4.8 percent, a figure that should be viewed in the context of the fact that taxes at this time claimed more than 60 percent of the Swedish GDP. There were, plain and simple, no margins in Swedish family budgets for what the austerity package did to their finances. It is therefore hardly surprising that over the three years, 1995–98, when the austerity package was imposed on them, Swedish consumers:[9]

- experienced no increase at all in their income—in 1998 total disposable household income was almost exactly the same, adjusted for inflation, as it was in 1993;

- kept their total spending on food and non-alcoholic beverages flat, in current prices—meaning they spent exactly the same amount of kronas at the grocery stores in 1998 as they did four years earlier, in 1994, the year before the austerity package came into effect;

- kept their spending on alcoholic beverages absolutely flat—and this in a country where alcohol has a prominent status in culture and culinary activities;

- increased spending on clothes and shoes by just about enough to keep up with inflation;

- cut their consumption, adjusted for inflation, of non-durable consumer products (including but not limited to food, beverages, cleaning supplies and home health and beauty products);

- kept their housing costs almost flat; at the time of this austerity package home construction had gone into a virtual standstill in Sweden; because of the non-existent supply of new homes, Swedish families could only keep their housing costs flat over four years by moving to less expensive housing.

In addition to depressing private consumption, the austerity package had a profoundly negative effect on household saving. In 1994, the year before the austerity purge, Swedish households put aside 61.8 billion kronas in savings; in 1998 they only saved 16 billion kronas, a drop of 74 percent. If we include other assets such as real estate, their savings dropped by a whopping 94 percent.[10]

9   Statistics Sweden, National Accounts Statistics. Available at: www.scb.se, accessed December 27, 2013.
10 Statistics Sweden, GDP by Income Components and Distribution by Sector. Available at: www. scb.se, accessed December 27, 2013.

Net savings excluding retirement savings dropped even further. In 1994 Swedish households set aside 4 percent of their income for non-retirement related net savings; in 1998 their non-retirement net savings had gone negative by 5 percent of household income.

This may sound like a technical detail, but it is a rather dramatic piece of information. As a direct result of the austerity policies, Swedish households went from building net worth, albeit slowly, to using credit cards and other forms of debt to keep their spending afloat. Alas, in 1994 Sweden's households had a total debt of 91 percent of their total disposable income; in 1998 that ratio had increased to 101.6 percent.

From a broader perspective this transformation of the Swede from a net saver to a net borrower is even more remarkable. The 1990 tax reform raised the cost of private consumption by massively expanding the value-added tax. It also lowered tax deductions related to debt while capping taxes on savings-derived income at a rate far lower than the top rate on employment-based income.

Figure 2.2   Sweden—employed, share of workforce

Source: Statistics Sweden, www.scb.se.

In other words: just after having created strong tax-based incentives for households to save, the Swedish government implemented an austerity package that made it practically impossible for people to save.

It is beyond question that Sweden's consumers were under immense pressure due to the austerity package. They kept key parts of their spending flat, with the result that businesses selling on the domestic market saw no real improvement in their bottom lines over the course of the austerity years. We can see this depressing effect of austerity in Figure 2.2, which illustrates the rate of employment in the 16–64 age group.

The blue function illustrates the employment rate. The following four points are important:

1.   The Swedish economy spent the 1980s recovering from the oil crises in the 1970s. A long growth period followed during which the economy reached its full-employment potential with an employment rate at 83 percent. After that peak point several variables coincided to cause a sharp downturn in 1990. The employment rate went into a tailspin: about 1 percent of the workforce lost their jobs every month for a year and a half.

2.   A turbulent few months in the summer and early fall of 1992 were followed by the end of the Swedish fixed exchange rate in November. The krona depreciated violently. In early 1993 Sweden's large manufacturing corporations, heavily dependent on foreign trade, slowly began picking up speed again. This stabilized the employment rate and the free-fall ended. There were signs of stabilization, but not a recovery, toward the end of 1994.

3.   In 1995 the social democrats, who won the 1994 election, began implementing the austerity package. Many key parts of consumer spending flattened out as a result, staying more or less flat for four years. This brought the employment rate recovery to an end and in fact made it decline somewhat.

4.   For the duration of the austerity package, 1995–98, the employment rate remained below 72 percent. This was 11 percent below the full-employment level reached before the recession.

If the story about the Swedish austerity period had ended here, it would not have been much different from the story of Greek, Spanish or Portuguese austerity. But unlike the disaster-stricken economies in today's Southern Europe, Sweden limped along and even experienced a minor recovery from the depth of the austerity years.

The reason was the nation's strong exports industry.

In the 1980s Swedish exports grew by an average of 4.4 percent per year, adjusted for inflation. In the 1990s the growth rate increased to 7.9 percent per year; in the "recovery years" of 1993–99, prior to the Millennium Recession, the annual growth rate was 9.6 percent per year. Sweden's exporters had a field day after the sharp 1992 depreciation of the Swedish currency.

As Figure 2.2 explained, this surge in exports did not translate into any recovery on the job market. All it did was to stabilize the employment rate. In fact, the jobs creation that resulted from the exports recovery was so weak that it was more than neutralized by the depressing effects of austerity on the jobs market.

It was not until the austerity years ended that the employment rate, as reported in Figure 2.2, actually started to increase. It was not a substantial increase, though: over the past decade the rate has stabilized at approximately 75 percent. A good 7 percent lower than the stable rate in the late 1980s, right before the crisis.

This persistently low employment rate is a very important piece in our understanding of what price the Swedish economy paid for its austerity years. At no time since the end of austerity has the Swedish economy been even close to its erstwhile employment rates from the 1980s. Statistically, 7 percent of the workforce has been left idling permanently.

This is a visible, tangible and permanent price that Sweden is paying for its austerity years. The policies of the austerity package undeniably cause a structural transformation of the economy. The transformation was either by design or by intent.

Behind the austerity package was one and only one policy directive: to balance the government budget. The road to accomplishing this did not go through growth-encouraging policies, but through the dark forests of tax hikes and spending cuts. The tax increases altered the rates at which people pay taxes at any given employment level—such as at the level where the economy was when the package was passed into law. Similarly, the spending cuts adjusted government outlays downward on a permanent basis, cutting expenses at any given employment level.

The result is visible in Figures 2.1 and 2.2 together: by the end of the austerity purge the Swedish government was able to balance its budget at an employment level 7 percent below its pre-crisis full employment level, when the budget was also in balance.

Since the goal with the austerity package was to balance the government budget, and since the social-democrat government achieved that goal at an employment rate far below full employment, there was in its view no need for any further policy measures to restore the 80+ percent employment levels of yore.

In a later chapter we will analyze the potential for combining a rising employment level with a closing of the budget deficit. This will require a radically different policy approach than the one the Swedes took.

Symptoms of Industrial Poverty

Again: the austerity package recalibrated the Swedish economy to feed the welfare state with its needed revenue without the need of 7 percent of the workforce.

Because the balanced budget was the policy goal of austerity, there was no incentive for the government to pursue policies for higher employment levels. Once the deficit was gone, the social-democrat administration rested on its laurels and focused on defending the budget balance.

For the Swedish public, though, the recalibration of the welfare state came with a heavy price tag. In addition to the lower permanent employment rate, they now paid a lot more in taxes and got much less back from government. If we think of the entitlements as a product that government produced and the public "purchased" through taxes, then 100 kronas worth of entitlements cost Swedish taxpayers:

- 76.70 kronas in 1994; but

- 93.72 kronas in 1998.

In other words, Swedish households experienced a 22 percent increase in the price of the entitlements they got from government. Regardless of one's personal opinion on entitlements and income redistribution, there is no doubt that this kind of net tax increase will take its toll on household finances. This increase also illustrates one of the great dangers with a welfare state, namely that when large segments of the population depend on tax-funded entitlements, there will be broadly felt repercussions when government can no longer pay for all the entitlements it has promised to people.

That said, it is worth noting the imbalance between tax input and entitlement consumption. Needless to say, when people pay 77 percent of the value of a product over a sustained period of time, somewhere else there is someone who directly and indirectly pays the balance. In the Swedish case corporate taxes chipped in the rest, forcing them to carry a tax burden that very likely could have eroded their productivity and, prior to the krona's deep depreciation in 1992, their ability to keep up with international competition.

Notably, though, the outcome of the austerity years was not a net reduction in the tax burden on the Swedish economy. It was a net tax increase. Part of that increase came in the form of a recalibration of the welfare state to make it fit within a smaller economy. But in addition to making the welfare state more costly to taxpayers, austerity also had consequences for the role of wages and salaries in household income. Because government no longer needed 7 percent of the workforce to pay for the welfare state's entitlements, almost 350,000 people were left idling without a job to go to. The private sector was operating under pressure from higher taxes and could therefore not re-create pre-crisis levels of employment.

As a result, Swedish households were forced to rely less on work-based income and more on income from investments (see Table 2.3).

Table 2.3   Composition of gross household income

	1995	2000	2005	2010
Wages and salaries	89.7%	79.7%	84.0%	83.6%
Income from business	2.7%	3.7%	4.1%	3.2%
Dividends and interest	5.8%	4.4%	3.6%	5.0%
Capital gains	1.8%	12.2%	8.3%	8.2%

Source: Statistics Sweden, www.scb.se.

Wages and salaries went from representing nine out of 10 kronas of income in 1995 to eight out of 10 in 2000. This is a remarkable drop, especially since it happened in a matter of a few short years. Equally remarkable is the rapid growth in capital gains, an income source that only plays a material role for a small segment of the population.

Two-thirds of the Swedish population have on average zero wealth,[11] and thus cannot rely on capital gains for their daily expenses. As a result, the depressed status of employment-based income reinforces the conclusion from the permanent drop in the employment rate that the Swedish economy has been permanently restructured by the 1990s austerity policies.

The depressed state of household finances after the austerity purge gave Sweden a big push in the direction of industrial poverty. The push would have been even stronger had it not been for the fact that Sweden's large, multinational manufacturing corporations experienced a surge in demand for their products on the global market. During the implementation of the austerity package the exports sector became the only part of the Swedish economy where profits and jobs were created (see Figure 2.3).[12]

Under less extreme economic conditions, it would not have been possible for exports to partly offset the drastically negative effects of an austerity package the size of 7 percent of GDP. Such spending cuts and tax increases would have been enough to crush any private sector. But corporations such as Volvo, Ericsson, SKF, ABB, Atlas Copco, SAAB, Alfa Laval, SCA and Sandvik took full advantage of the depressed Swedish krona to gain advantages on big exports markets. They were also helped along by the moderating effects on labor costs that resulted from very high unemployment. Lastly, their sales on the Swedish market were for the most part so minuscule compared to their exports that they were immune to the depression of domestic demand in the Swedish economy.

---

11 Statistics Sweden, GDP by Income Components and Distribution by Sector. Available at: www. scb.se, accessed December 27, 2013.

12 These are fixed-price figures. It is preferable to measure GDP shares in current prices, as that more accurately reflects the real-life situation of actual economic agents. However, for a long-term overview such as the one reported here, the difference between fixed and current prices is not of decisive importance. The point about private consumption falling below 50 percent of GDP is still valid.

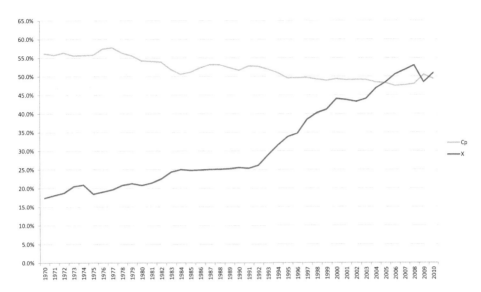

Figure 2.3   Exports and private consumption
Source: United Nations National Accounts Data, www.un.org.

The surge in exports rapidly increased profits in export-dominated corporations, leading their stocks to perform well. Dividends and capital gains rose dramatically.

As a result, government experienced a spike in tax revenues. This accelerated the recovery of the budget without the need for nearly the number of jobs required to restore pre-crisis employment levels.

The surge in exports after 1992 permanently shifted the balance between private consumption and exports. During the growth-dominated 1980s exports accounted for one quarter of the Swedish GDP; by 1998 that share had grown to 40 percent. It kept growing, exceeding 50 percent in 2006 and has remained at that level since then.

During the period when exports have surged in importance, private consumption has slowly reduced its role in the economy. By 1995 it fell below 50 percent and has basically remained there since then. In the aftermath of the 1990s austerity policies, the Swedish economy leapt from being a traditional industrialized economy where most of the production is oriented toward domestic needs to an economy that critically depends on international trade to maintain employment, profits and tax revenues.

Which brings us back to Figures 2.2 and 2.1 in that order. According to Figure 2.2, after the austerity policies end in 1998 there is a rise in the employment rate again. The exports industry has already added jobs, so this rise is caused by an easing of the austerity pressure on consumers' finances. In short: once the fiscally oppressive austerity policies ended, Sweden's consumers moderately increased their spending and created just enough demand for more jobs to bring the employment rate up from 72 to 75 percent.

This part of the Swedish austerity experience confirms one critical point made earlier about industrial poverty, namely that a country with a big welfare state cannot use exports to pull itself out of a deep recession. Today the Spanish government has invested hope in exports to provide a turnaround for the depressed economy, a scenario that, with the Swedish experience as a background, is very unlikely to happen.

Figure 2.3 also tells us that Swedish household consumption dropped below 50 percent of GDP during the austerity years and has not recovered since then. This is one indicator that Sweden has gotten stuck in a state of industrial poverty. As for the inflation-adjusted growth rate of private consumption, over the last decade it has stayed just above 2 percent per year.[13] Technically, this indicates that Sweden is not yet a country in industrial poverty. However, one way of deepening the test of industrial poverty is to measure the growth in inflation-adjusted private consumption compared to the growth in household indebtedness. If household debt grows over time while consumption continues to grow at more than 2 percent, we have reasons to believe that households are unable to maintain a standard of living above industrial poverty on the merits of their own, current incomes.

We mentioned Swedish private-sector indebtedness earlier: during the austerity years household debt grew from 91 percent of disposable income to 101 percent. After a couple of years of debt-to-income stability the rate took off again after the Millennium Recession: households accelerated their debt from 113.3 percent of disposable income in 2002 to 169 percent in 2010. Much of this indebtedness is related to mortgage loans, but mortgages play a relatively important role in funding consumption in Sweden. In fact, recently the IMF criticized Sweden for policies that have encouraged disturbingly high levels of debt among the general public.[14]

---

13 Measuring rolling 10-year averages.
14 *Executive Board Article IV Consultation with Sweden*; International Monetary Fund, September 2013. Available at: http://www.imf.org/external/np/sec/pr/2013/pr13325.htm, accessed December 27, 2013.

This is not the place to discuss household credit policies per se, but it is worth noting that Sweden's households have not been able to continue to grow their consumption solely out of their disposable income. On the contrary, between 1997 and 2007 consumption grew faster than disposable income in eight years out of 10. Had consumption instead grown on par with disposable income, the average consumption growth rate would have been below 2 percent per year for most of that period.

If there is doubt about Sweden in terms of private consumption growth, there is no question that the third test variable classifies Sweden as an economy in industrial poverty. Since 2004 youth unemployment has been above 20 percent every year except 2007 (when it was 19.2 percent). Since the Great Recession started the Swedish youth unemployment rate has been hovering close to 25 percent, showing no signs of decline.

While we can tie the tepid growth in private consumption back to the austerity policies of the 1990s (via the structurally lower employment rate) it is not as obvious that the very high rate of youth unemployment has any connection back to those years. Indirectly, though, there is a connection: the reason why a smaller share of the workforce is employed (with the employment rate at 75 percent) is that there are fewer jobs per 100 working-age people in general. The flip side of this lower employment rate is higher unemployment. When unemployment becomes persistent over time, it hits the young and inexperienced harder than highly skilled workers.

There is one more aspect to the Swedish crisis: big government. It is relevant both as an explanatory factor behind the crisis and, as the next chapter explains, in our understanding of whether or not Sweden is in a state of industrial poverty.

In common conversations on public policy, Sweden is almost the definition of big government. There is plenty of evidence to show that the Swedish government indeed is one of the absolutely largest in the world. Figure 2.4 reports total government spending and revenue as share of GDP from the cusp of the 1990s crisis through the austerity years, the Millennium Recession and right up to the point where the current recession begins.

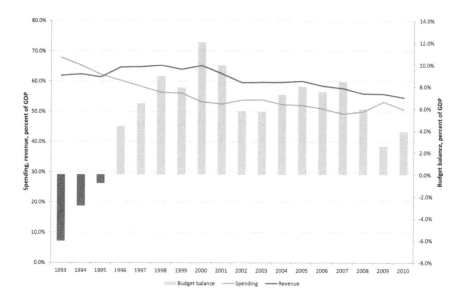

Figure 2.4   Total government spending, revenue and balance
Source: Statistics Sweden, www.scb.se.

Unlike Figure 2.1, which only represents the national government, Figure 2.4 reports numbers for the entire government sector: national, regional, local and the large general income security system. Government spending exceeds 50 percent of GDP for the entire period displayed, with revenue exceeding spending by a big margin starting in 1996.

For reasons that the next chapter elaborates on, when government spending exceeds 40 percent of GDP the economy enters a path toward stagnation and industrial poverty. At that point, private consumption growth falls short of 2 percent per year, another important threshold for industrial poverty.

Does Sweden exhibit a correlation between big government and very low growth rates in private consumption? At first glance, it looks like the answer is no. It seems as though Sweden's consumers have been able to stay above the 2 percent growth mark. Consider the numbers in the middle column of Table 2.4. This table reports inflation-adjusted growth rates in private consumption as 10-year averages: every year's number represents an average for 10 years. The figure for 2003 in the middle column, 2.6 percent, represents an average for the 10-year period 1994–2003; the number for 2004 is the average for the period 1995–2004, etc. (Yearly reports of 10-year averages give a sense of stability and trend to the data.)

Table 2.4   Private consumption

Growth rates, fixed prices		
	Actual	**Adjusted**
2003	2.6%	0.0%
2004	2.7%	-0.7%
2005	2.8%	-1.4%
2006	2.9%	-1.9%
2007	3.0%	-2.1%
2008	2.7%	-1.5%
2009	2.2%	-0.6%
2010	2.2%	0.2%
2011	2.3%	0.5%
2012	2.2%	0.9%

Source: Statistics Sweden, www.scb.se.

As mentioned earlier, the problem for Sweden's households is, as mentioned earlier, that ever since the 1990s austerity campaign they have taken on massive new debt. Between the end of the austerity years and the beginning of the current crisis Swedish households have increased their debt from about 100 percent to 169 percent of their disposable income.

This means, in short, that they have funded a large part of their consumption with borrowed money. With growing debt come growing debt payments, which thus consume more and more of their disposable income. Current consumption is pushed aside, forcing consumers to freeze and eventually reduce their standard of living.

If we assume that household borrowing had stayed constant as a ratio to disposable income, the numbers from Table 2.3 mid-column would look quite different, as reported in the right column: six out of 10 reported averages are now negative, and one is exactly at 0 percent. Not one average exceeds 1 percent.

Overall the Swedish consumer is now a far cry from increasing his consumption at 2 percent per year. He does not come close to the threshold above which he has to be in order to stay out of industrial poverty.

In other words, we can conclude that the Swedish government is big enough to depress the economy, that it brings about economic stagnation and forces consumers to go deep into debt just to maintain an illusion of a stable standard of living.

A major reason why the Swedish economy is de facto in a state of stagnation is that government, big and vast, is consistently running a large surplus. Returning again to Figure 2.4, the reported surpluses, with a start in 1996, average an astounding 7 percent of GDP. This means that 8 kronas out of every 100 kronas that Swedes pay in taxes go straight into government coffers—and remain there.

There is a correlation between this relentless pursuit of a budget surplus and the fact that Swedish consumers are counting on debt to keep their standard of living going. In 1996 consumers increased their borrowing by 20.9 billion kronas, or one quarter of the total government surplus. In 2008 consumer borrowing equaled 92 percent of the total government surplus.

To sum up the Swedish crisis:

- a regular recession was aggravated by a real estate crisis, putting banks in a difficult situation;

- the crisis caused a big budget deficit which exposed a structural imbalance between tax revenues that paid for the welfare state and entitlement spending;

- the social-democrat government decided to close the budget deficit by means of a large, tough austerity package amounting to 7 percent of GDP;

- the package recalibrated the welfare state so it could get enough revenue for its spending at a much lower economic activity rate than before the crisis;

- as a result of the austerity policies, private consumption slowed down, household saving stopped and households went deep into debt;

- for a while during the crisis government consumed and taxed more than 60 percent of GDP;

- the Swedish economy would have been even worse off were it not for partial help from the large exports sector.

The lingering question, then, is whether or not the crisis and its flawed austerity remedy sunk Sweden into a permanent state of industrial poverty. To answer this question, we must first explore the concept of industrial poverty a bit closer. Then we can move on to ask: could Sweden have done better under a different kind of austerity program?

Chapter 3

Industrial Poverty

It is an inescapable fact that Europe's welfare state is part of its current problems. Over its decades-long life, the welfare state has fundamentally transformed large parts of the economic landscape. It has changed the motivation for people to work, from building personal finances to paying taxes. It has altered the motives for participating in the workforce by providing tax-paid entitlements that pay for an assortment of people's basic needs. Its redistribution policies discourage entrepreneurship and encourage sloth and indolence and take the edge off the rewards for pursuing high-end professional careers.

When the welfare state grows past a certain point, its influence on the economy becomes overall negative. It jeopardizes, and eventually seriously weakens, the human urges that provide the fuel for growth and the pursuit of prosperity. In a manner of speaking, its economic incentives are biased toward comfort and rest, not toward motion and growth.

As a result, when the economy grinds to a halt it therefore lacks many of the mechanisms that would pull an economy without an oversized government out of its recession.

It is not a coincidence that the U.S. economy was slowly recovering in the spring 2013 while the European economy was still looking at stagnation and mass unemployment. It is also no coincidence that the implementation of the Affordable Care Act—aka, Obamacare—has a negative effect on private-sector economic activity. The American welfare state is still relatively limited compared to its European counterparts, yet it remains to be seen what effect the Affordable Care Act will have in that respect.

While it is always important to debate the merits and demerits of a welfare state, available evidence suggests that Europe's crisis originates in an oversized welfare state. This leads to another suggestion, namely that Europe will never recover so long as its political leaders insist on preserving the welfare state.

So far that is exactly what they have done: their austerity policies have aimed at adjusting the welfare state to what the private sector can afford. Austerity is, in effect, a form of recalibration of the welfare state. This was its consequence in Sweden, and this is its consequence in Europe today. However, the recalibration itself does permanent damage by costing millions of jobs and by drawing legislative attention away from full employment and growth. Instead, lawmakers become entirely focused on balancing the budget. This in turn puts more destructive pressure on the private sector and in fact makes it more difficult for the welfare state and the private sector to coexist within the same economy.

On May 31, 2013, the British newspaper the *Guardian* reported on a telling example of what this destructive coexistence can lead to:[1]

> *Wages have fallen across Spain in the past year as the government tries to cheapen labour for employers just as austerity measures cut back the welfare state. Salaries fell by an average of 0.6% in the year to the first quarter, with inflation pushing the real loss in the purchasing power of those Spaniards in work to 2%. Private sector salaries were harder hit than those of public employees.*

This comes at a point in time when the Spanish unemployment rate has reached 27 percent.

There is nothing inherently wrong with wages taking a nosedive in a recession: the wage is the price of labor and if labor is in excess supply the price needs to fall as part of the free-market adjustment process to restore full employment. Apparently, as the *Guardian* reports, the Spanish prime minister believes that the decline in workers' earnings in his country is due to a sound market-based adjustment of the price of labor:

> *Falling wages are seen as good news by prime minister Mariano Rajoy's conservative People's party government, which believes wage devaluation is one of the few options left to Spain now it is part of the euro and can no longer devalue its own currency. "This will help us become more competitive," the country's employer's federation said.*

---

1   "Spanish wages depressed amid Eurozone crisis," *Guardian*, May 31, 2013. Available at: http://www.guardian.co.uk/world/2013/may/31/spanish-wages-depressed-eurozone-crisis, accessed December 27, 2013.

The problem for Mr. Rajoy is that this is not the result of a purely market-driven process. Just like in Sweden in the 1990s this program includes both higher taxes and cuts in government spending, an attempt by the Spanish government to downsize its welfare state to fit a smaller private sector. But just as in Sweden, the end result is a government that takes more from the private sector and gives less back. This depresses private-sector activity, paving the way for the very high unemployment rates we see in many European countries today.

Since unemployment is driving wages down, the real reason for the wage drop is that the Spanish government wants to preserve its welfare state—not that it wants an economy where free-market principles rule.

From Austerity to Industrial Poverty

Taxes are now higher than before austerity; government offers downsized services and entitlements compared to before austerity; and now wages are beginning to fall. Taken together, these are indicators of a sustained decline in the standard of living for Spanish families. There are many signs that most of Europe is joining Spain, to a larger or lesser degree, in that decline. The decline, accelerated by austerity, is the beginning of a new economic phase.

Industrial poverty.

This new form of poverty is not the kind experienced by too many hundreds of millions of people in undeveloped parts of the world. It allows people to enjoy the basic conveniences of an industrialized society:

- running water and power and heat in homes that are reasonably comfortable but cramped and lacking modern architectural solutions;

- reliable retail supply of basic groceries and clothes, but higher-quality products that most of us are used to being able to buy will be exclusive for the very few with a little more money to spend;

- access to transportation services including small, cheap cars for those who can afford them;

- health care that offers good chances of surviving the most common diseases but not a cure for more advanced medical conditions;

- a static standard of living where children, at best, grow up to the same kind of life their parents had.

This is pretty much what life was like in Eastern Europe during the Soviet era. Stagnant, static, without a future worth striving for. Under the Soviet economic model, there was no way for anyone to earn a better life by working harder and excelling at a career. Building a business was basically the same as treason. As a result, no one could advance their private finances or improve their standard of living.

All of these barriers to a better life were forcefully imposed by the communists as part of their ideological desire to create a synthetic society. Under industrial poverty there are no such hindrances to success. All people are free to make more money and raise their standard of living. But unlike life under economic freedom, people cannot cut their own path from poverty to prosperity by means of ingenuity, entrepreneurship and hard work.

The biggest obstacle is a permanently stagnant economy. In statistical terms, this means a GDP that is barely growing at all—a good estimate is less than 2 percent in "good" economic times and 0 percent on average over a business cycle. There is general agreement in the macroeconomic literature that an economy needs to grow by at least 2 percent per year to reduce unemployment and allow people to improve their standard of living.[2] When GDP gets stuck at growth rates below 2 percent, and averages out at a statistical standstill over a business cycle, there will be no improvement whatsoever in people's prospects, either on the job market or in terms of ever improving their daily lives.

We refer to this stagnation as industrial poverty, a state of economic affairs that we can identify using the four variables mentioned earlier:

- stagnation in private consumption;

- the decline in private consumption as an important economic variable;

---

2   There is a wealth of academic literature on this subject. For a popularized version, please see: http://finance.yahoo.com/news/okuns-law-economic-growth-unemployment-203855211.html, accessed December 27, 2013.

- high youth unemployment; and

- oversized government.

Variable 1: Stagnant Private Consumption

When the overall economy, GDP, grows at less than 2 percent over time, it almost automatically means that private consumption will grow by less than 2 percent. This gives us a good "street level" indicator of how deeply into industrial poverty a country has sunk.

Private consumption is a good indicator of how well-to-do we are as a nation. It covers our purchases of everything from necessities such as food, clothes, housing and transportation to pure luxuries such as a new Mercedes or a dinner at a five-star restaurant. Therefore, when private consumption growth averages 2 percent or less over time, it is an indicator of structural stagnation, that is, industrial poverty.

Swedish data, when adjusted for a relentlessly rising ratio of household debt to GDP, showed a country deeply into a state of industrial poverty.

When consumption grows at 2 percent or less, adjusted for inflation, our standard of living is stagnant or in decline. This may seem counter-intuitive—after all, when consumption grows we are spending more in real terms, are we not?

Arithmetically, that is correct. However, the real world does not always confine itself to the strict definitions of mathematics. There are phenomena in our lives, and especially in our economy, that do not allow themselves to be easily captured with mathematical precision.

As consumers we spend money on a wide variety of things, from simple consumer goods like dish detergent to complex services like legal advice. Over time, we maintain a fairly stable "basket" of goods and services that we purchase with varying regularity.

We spend about the same shares of our income on food, housing, clothes and daily transportation today as we did two or three decades ago. In most industrialized countries these four categories make up 60–65 percent of consumer spending.

While it is easy to get the impression that a steady standard of living is the same as spending the exact same amount on those basic items over time, the fact of the matter is that the products we buy get slightly better each year. The basic car that most people buy gets a little better, with new features, higher quality materials and better fuel economy. Our standard grocery bag gets a little better, with higher-quality raw materials and more food products being produced on environmentally friendly terms.

The same goes for the services we buy. Even though we use the same tax accountant every year, his skills and knowledge of tax law has to get a little better each year to allow him to keep up with changes to tax law. When we go on our regular summer vacation trip, which involves staying at the same hotels, eating at the same restaurants and going to the same fun parks, we often see improvements that increase the quality of the experience, even if just on the margin.

When products get a little better we normally have to pay a little more for them. This higher cost is represented by an annual 2 percent increase in private consumption: when we increase our inflation-adjusted household spending by approximately 2 percent per year we do so merely to keep up with the quality evolution of the products that make up our basic standard of living.

Okun's Law and Private Consumption

But how do we conclude that quality advancements cost us about 2 percent per year? To answer that question we apply a nifty instrument from economics called Okun's law. Named after prominent economist Arthur Okun, this law suggests a regular relationship between unemployment and GDP growth. When GDP grows at a certain percent per year, or less, unemployment will not fall and might go up instead.[3]

There is no absolute, universally applicable growth rate for GDP in Okun's law, though many estimates point to approximately 2 percent. Recent studies suggest that GDP might actually have to grow by as much as 3 percent per year before unemployment begins to fall.[4]

---

3   For an excellent but scholarly presentation of Okun's law, see: Thirlwall, A.P., "Okun's law and the natural rate of growth," *Southern Economic Journal* Vol. 36, July 1969.
4   Higgins, P., "GDP growth, the unemployment rate and Okun's law," EconSouth, Federal Reserve Bank of Atlanta, 2011; available at: http://www.frbatlanta.org/documents/pubs/

So what does this have to do with the quality evolution of our private consumption?

Here is how it works. There are two reasons why unemployment does not fall when GDP grows by about 2 percent per year: the labor force continues to grow; and technology advancements allow for more to be produced by a constant workforce. The advancement in technology is in good part translated into higher-quality consumer products; in services, the analogy to technological advancements is higher skills and better education of the professionals who produce those services. (Okun's study that led to the definition of the law covered data from 1947 to 1960. At that time services were a smaller part of our economy than they are today.)

Labor forces in modern industrialized economies grow by, approximately, 1 percent per year. If Okun's law requires a GDP growth rate of up to 3 percent for unemployment to fall, it is fair to conclude that 2 percent of that GDP growth comes from general technological advancements and improved skills in manufacturing as well as education—human capital—in services industries. Therefore, we can also conclude that the items we spend money on as consumers will cost 2 percent more each year to reflect the improvement in quality.

This means, again, that when private consumption increases at no more than 2 percent per year, adjusted for inflation, we are really only maintaining the same standard of living as before. We need to grow our consumption by more than that to raise our standard of living.

Figure 3.1 illustrates the annual average growth rates in inflation-adjusted private consumption in 15 industrialized countries over the period 2000–2010.

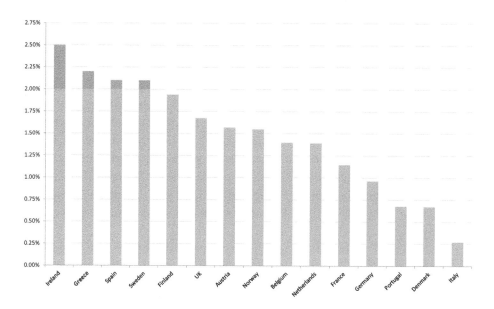

Figure 3.1   Consumption growth
Source: United Nations National Accounts, www.un.org.

These growth rates are not adjusted for household debt, which makes the several observations of below-2 percent growth even more compelling.

During this period, which only covers the opening of the Great Recession, only four countries managed to raise themselves above the 2 percent per year level. In a recession, consumption obviously grows more slowly than in good economic times; the best way to gauge whether or not we are spending just to maintain our stagnant standard of living is to do it when the economy is considered strong. That was the case both in the United States and in Europe for the better part of the period 2000–2010. Alas, according to this variable, most of the sampled countries were in fact in a state of industrial poverty.

Furthermore, the margins in the four countries above 2 percent are so small that a sustained recession will push the average down into industrial poverty territory. Again, while a recession should not be the defining period for an assessment of whether or not a country is in fact sinking into industrial poverty, it is also telling of the weakness of an economy if it remains in a prolonged recession.

Spain is a case in point: the recession has now reached such drastic proportions that compensation of employees in the private sector is falling.

Wages are notoriously sticky downward in modern economies. There is a plethora of reasons for this, some of which have been eminently established by Yale economics professor Truman Bewley.[5] It takes formidable pressure from a deep, long crisis and very high unemployment before individual and institutional resistance to pay cuts is overwhelmed. The fact that Spain has now reached this point is yet another indicator that this is no usual crisis.

Let me again make clear that there is nothing inherently wrong with wages falling. While there is a natural gravitation toward price stability in a free-market economy, it is also natural for prices to adjust quickly and completely when the conditions for such stability change. In other words, so long as an economy is free of government incursions its prices will stabilize and adjust exclusively as a result of rational decisions by buyers and sellers.

The problem with wage reductions in Europe today is that they do not happen under free-market terms. The wage cuts will translate into lasting reductions in real purchasing power, one consequence of which is stagnant private consumption.

Europe's economies are by no means free. Government typically runs 40–50 percent of GDP through its budgets by taxing and spending, and eagerly regulates the rest of the economy. The labor market is particularly heavily burdened by regulations. In the Index of Economic Freedom, published annually by the Heritage Foundation, the most crisis-ridden EU member states rank poorly in terms of labor market freedom: Spain scores 54.3, compared to 95.5 by world-leading United States; Italy is at 52.0; Greece scores 42.1 and Portugal comes in at an abysmal 31.0.[6]

It is practically impossible for the free-market price mechanism to have anything but marginal influence on worker compensation. When wages do begin to fall, though, there will be a marginally positive reaction in the form of more jobs. However, due to the increased presence of government in the economy, as a result of austerity, it is unreasonable to expect that positive effect to make any noticeable difference to the Spanish unemployment rate.

The reason why there will be only a marginal upturn is related to our next variable for defining industrial poverty.

---

5   Bewley, T., *Why Wages Don't Fall During a Recession*, Harvard University Press, Cambridge, MA, 2002.
6   Please see: http://www.heritage.org/index/explore, accessed December 27, 2013.

Variable 2: Insignificant Private Consumption

The only sector that can benefit from lower wages is the exports industry. Some of Europe's political leaders, such as the Spanish prime minister, are hoping that exports will save the day and lead the way back to more prosperous times.

In theory, growing exports will benefit the rest of the economy by means of multiplier effects. Thriving exporting businesses create more jobs, newly employed people spend more—increase their private consumption—helping revive the domestic sector. This Keynesian argument, founded in the well-documented multiplier, would under normal macroeconomic conditions have great merit. However, in a structural crisis that has been aggravated by austerity the economy's normal reaction patterns have been upset. The degree of uncertainty is higher, discouraging more spending. But even more significant is the combined effect of uncertainty and falling money wages: together the higher net drainage by government and the reduced purchasing power will outweigh any positive multiplier effects.

But should not a fall in wages lead to a surge in exports and a decline in unemployment? What about the economic success stories in Eastern Asia, from Japan in the 1960s and 1970s to China in the past 20 years? Exports have been the driving force in those economic growth wonders.

The problem for Europe is that the situation is markedly different. Japan, South Korea, China and other Asian tiger economies did not have a big welfare state in place when they began their quest for prosperity by means of exports. Europe today is mired in stagnation because of the welfare state and the austerity policies aimed at saving it. The large burden on the private sector imposed by the welfare state is still there and will not change just because exporting businesses are thriving. The extra net drainage from the private sector caused by austerity will not go down.

When people have to pay higher taxes and when they see that austerity has eroded what they can expect to get back from the economy (health care rationing, lower or eliminated medical subsidies, cuts in college tuition subsidies, lower benefits in case they lose their jobs) their first reaction is not going to be to spend more money on nice shirts, a new car or better-looking furniture. Their first reaction is going to be to set aside as much money as they can in the event that they, too, lose their jobs, to send their kids to college or to buy unsubsidized medicine.

In macroeconomic theory this is called a drop in the propensity to consume. The combination of a lower propensity to consume and higher taxes significantly weakens the multiplier. The mechanism that was expected to spread better times from the exports industry to the rest of the economy will not do nearly as good a job as it would have done before the crisis began. There are going to be some multiplier effects that benefit retail, the services industry and domestic-selling manufacturers, but it is extremely unlikely that any of the European economies hit by austerity will climb back to pre-recession levels of employment and per-capita GDP simply by depressing wages and relying on exports. Again, Sweden is a much better object of comparison than the Asian tiger economies.

Again: from a free-market viewpoint it does not matter whether a business in Europe sells its products to its neighbors, to Japanese buyers or to customers on the Klingon home world. But Europe's problem in general, and Spain's in particular, is that bad government policy is depressing domestic economic activity and causing wages to drop so that domestic-oriented businesses are disadvantaged over exporting businesses. Government policies aiming to save a morbidly obese welfare state tilt the playing field in favor of one type of business—the exporter—and against another type, namely that which sells to their neighbors and fellow countrymen.

We can actually see these effects play out in national accounts data. Countries with big welfare states that try to export themselves to prosperity have a high share of exports in their GDP. If the effect of the welfare state is as described here, namely that ...

- austerity drives up unemployment;

- unemployment depresses wages; and

- the combined effect is a depression of domestic spending, primarily private consumption

... then we should see a trend over time where private consumption is declining as share of GDP.

There are two ways to illustrate this decline. One is to simply calculate the consumption percentage of GDP; the other is to calculate a ratio between private consumption and exports. A country is in industrial poverty if:

- private consumption is below 50 percent of GDP; and

- private consumption is smaller than exports.

If government does not have a depressing effect on the domestic economy, then large exports should correlate with large private consumption. If on the other hand government depresses people's take-home wages by forcing up unemployment and imposing heavy taxes, then large exports should correlate with small private consumption.

The grey bars in Figure 3.2 illustrate the average annual rate of private consumption to GDP in 15 European countries.[7]

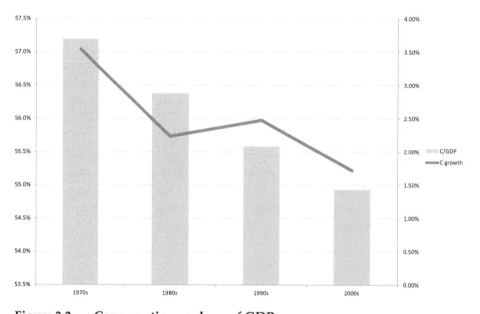

Figure 3.2   Consumption as share of GDP
Source: United Nations National Accounts database; Eurostat GDP data.

Focusing again for a moment exclusively on the grey bars, we see an inevitable trend of decline in the ratio of private consumption to GDP. On average it has

---

7   Austria, Belgium, Denmark, Finland, France, Germany, Greece, Ireland, Italy, the Netherlands, Norway, Portugal, Spain, Sweden and the United Kingdom. These countries were selected for two reasons: they are all European and there was consistency in access to data.

dropped from 57.2 percent for these 15 European countries in the 1970s to 54.9 percent in the 2000s.

Before we look at exports, does this mean that we have identified 15 countries en route to industrial poverty? Not necessarily, but there is clearly a danger of that. For comparison, Figure 3.2 also displays the average growth rate in private consumption for the same countries during the same time period. The black line reveals a downward trend in this variable as well, with the average for the 2000s being 1.7 percent, half of what it was in the 1970s.

It seems like we have a group of countries here that already before the current crisis were on a long-term path to industrial poverty. To find more evidence, let us take a look at the other part of our Variable 2, namely the exports share of GDP (see Figure 3.3).

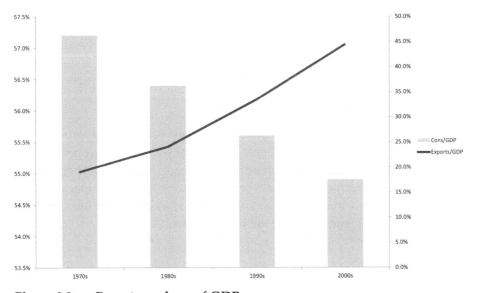

Figure 3.3   Exports as share of GDP
Source: United Nations National Accounts data, www.un.org.

Figures 3.2 and 3.3 clearly show a correlation between:

- a declining growth rate in consumption;

- a falling share of GDP being spent on consumption; and

- a growing share of GDP going toward exports.

The low consumption growth rate—on average below 2 percent per year in the 2000s for this group of 15 countries—is the most obvious sign that people are not becoming better off. Exports cannot pull an economy out of a recession caused by big government.

Until this conclusion sinks in to the minds of policy-makers in Europe, the crisis is going to prevail. As it does, it continues to destroy Europe's very social and economic fabric. When people lose hope of a better tomorrow, and when years go by without them being able to regain that hope, people become dispirited and disillusioned.

In a normal recession this would be a source of innovation and creativity. People would try out new entrepreneurial endeavors, start new businesses and venture into the realm where dedication, hard work and the animal spirit make the difference. But this is not a normal recession: the cause is not a slump in the business cycle like any other. The cause is instead a structurally intrusive government that stifles business activity in general. But high taxes and onerous regulations, especially on the labor market (for which Europe is notorious), impose a much higher fixed-cost burden on small businesses than on large corporations.

This together with a deeply depressed domestic economy places a big wall of discouragement in the way of entrepreneurially minded Europeans. This adds insult to injury for large chunks of working-age Europeans, especially the young, who find themselves out of work much more often than older workers. This is particularly troublesome, since the young workers are the ones who are supposed to inherit and take over today's economy.

Variable 3: Youth Unemployment

The longer young people go without work, the more difficult it becomes for them to come out as net contributors to the economy over their lifespan. The more young people who go unemployed, the poorer an entire generation becomes.

High, persistent unemployment among the young puts the economy on a path to generational decline: the growing generation will be poorer than the generation of its parents.

Generational decline is yet another symptom of industrial poverty. However, it is thus far difficult to measure; a good proxy is the more easily identifiable rate of youth unemployment.

By the end of 2012, two out of three EU member states—a total of 19—had a youth unemployment rate above 20 percent.[8] As of the first quarter of 2013, average youth unemployment in the EU is 24.1 percent. This is an increase of 1.1 percentage points compared to the first quarter of 2012. In one year, Europe's struggling economies added 150,000 young people registered to the unemployment rosters.

While the youth unemployment rate in the United States remains steady at around 16.6 percent, the rate in Europe is increasing, in many cases to disturbingly high levels. In some countries in our group of 15, the rate is downright alarming (see Table 3.1).

Table 3.1   Youth unemployment, first quarter 2013 (first quarter 2012)

Greece	60.3 (52.7)	Belgium	22.4 (18.8)
Spain	57.2 (52.0)	Denmark	13.5 (15.5)
Portugal	42.1 (36.2)	Netherlands	11.1 (9.9)
Italy	41.9 (35.9)	Norway	9.3 (7.6)
Ireland	27.2 (29.7)	Germany	7.8 (8.0)
France	27.1 (23.8)	U.K.	20.4 (21.4)
Sweden	26.4 (24.9)	Austria	8.1 (8.9)
Finland	2.4 (21.7)		

Source: Eurostat. Methodological note: Quarterly data for Q1, 2013, for Austria and the United Kingdom were not available at the time of writing. The table reports numbers for Q4, 2012. Since these are not seasonally adjusted numbers, this makes the comparison with other countries imperfect.

To make matters worse, in some countries this is not a new phenomenon (see Table 3.2).

---

8   Please see Eurostat Unemployment Statistics at: http://epp.eurostat.ec.europa.eu/portal/page/
     portal/employment_unemployment_lfs/data/database, accessed December 27, 2013.

Table 3.2   Youth unemployment, averages per decade (full series not available for all countries)

	1980s	1990s	2000s
Belgium	18.8	20.5	20.5
Denmark	10.6	8.8	10.3
Germany	–	9.3	11.5
Ireland	22.7	14.4	16.8
Greece	–	–	30.8
Spain	–	–	30.4
France	17.3	20.9	21.7
Italy	27.9	27.4	25.2
Netherlands	8.7	8.2	8.0
Austria	–	6.0	9.0
Portugal	15.3	13.5	23.8
Finland	14.3	25.8	19.6
Sweden	6.9	17.5	21.8
U.K.	15.2	14.0	16.1

Source: Eurostat.

Corresponding numbers for Norway for the 1990s and 2000s are, respectively, 10.9 and 9.3 percent.

As is evident from Tables 3.1 and 3.2, youth unemployment is a long-time problem for Europe. Despite the glitches in data reporting, we can see a slow upward trend in the numbers: the average reported youth unemployment rate per reporting country was 15.8 percent in the 1980s and 18.3 percent in the 2000s.

This long-time upward trend is a significant indicator of looming industrial poverty. When more than 20 percent of the young are unemployed on a sustained basis, the young generation begins to lose its ability to replace the older as producers of prosperity.

The longer the young are unemployed, the shorter is the time that they will be active as producers and taxpayers in the economy. There comes a point when at an individual level the balance between being a taker of government entitlements and a funder of those same entitlements is shifted into the negative.

Retirement funding is one good example. In most European welfare states an individual has to be employed for approximately 40 years to fund his own retirement with his own taxes. When citizens aged 25 or younger are unemployed at rates in excess of 20 percent, one-fifth of the workforce is (at least in theory) going to need others to contribute to their retirement.

The reason why the 20 percent threshold matters has to do with workforce participation. In good economic times, when GDP growth has been at high levels, Europe's welfare states have seen workforce participation rates up to 80 percent.[9] Those levels have sustained the funding of the welfare state until work-discouraging taxes and entitlements brought that rate down. If at least 80 percent of the young are "paying for themselves" through their work career, in terms of welfare-state entitlements and the retirement system, then since the welfare state has historically sustained at that workforce participation rate, they will also be contributing enough to pay for the net cost that the remaining 20 percent inflict on the welfare state.

Because of the long-term depressing effect of the welfare state on private consumption, GDP growth and jobs creation, the workforce participation rate will inevitably decline. As it does, the cost to taxpayers for those who do not work increases almost logarithmically. The cost of government goes up over time, causing, for example, a slow but inevitable rise in youth unemployment.

This is exactly what has been happening in Europe over the past three decades. During the same time the European economies have slowly shifted away from being consumption-based to being exports-based and toward funding an increasingly unsustainable welfare state.

And Then Came the Neeters

Europe has been on a long-term path to slow growth and economic stagnation, but up until the Great Recession it has maintained at least an appearance of business-as-usual. However, the recent years of crisis have put the continent on a downbound path into industrial poverty.

One of the most pressing problems for Europe is its sky-high youth unemployment. As the numbers in Table 3.2 indicate, having high rates of unemployment among the young is nothing new to this recession. The news

---

9   Please see Workforce Participation Statistics by the International Labor Organization. Available at: www.ilo.org, accessed December 27, 2013.

is instead in the overall picture of Europe, where high—and rising—youth unemployment is one important piece.

High, sustained levels of unemployment detach the young from society and the economy. In the footsteps of detachment follow apathy, indifference and eventually, after many years, frustration over what is turning into a squandered life.

As part of an effort to understanding what this means on a broader scale, we can take a look at the so-called neeter phenomenon. We begin with a tour back to 2004 and an article in the British daily newspaper the *Guardian*:[10]

> For most people, the suggestion that a sizeable number of British teenagers has a neet problem will prompt images of strong hair lotions and fine-tooth combs. A Japanese team of researchers that came over to Sheffield recently knows different, because their nation has neets too. The number of young Japanese not in education, employment or training – the neets – is now [in 2004] an estimated 600,000. The scale of Britain's neet phenomenon is difficult to gauge … a report by the Social Exclusion Unit … found that "at any one time, 161,000, or 9%, of the age group [16–19] are outside of education, training and work for long periods after the school-leaving age of 16."

The neeter problem emerged in Japan as a result of the long, dragged-out 1990s recession. The economy grew very slowly and produced too few opportunities for young people to build a life on their own. As a result, researchers began defining the neeter problem toward the end of the 1990s.

In Britain in 2004 the neeter problem was even more pervasive. With an unemployment rate of 12.1 percent at the time, British youth faced a considerably tougher challenge than their Japanese peers when it came to finding a job. As a result, according to the *Guardian* story, the neeters in Britain tend to be low-educated, with little or no academic tradition in the family.

The point with identifying the neeters is that it reinforces the impression of a lost generation, whose standard of living will be lower than that which their parents enjoy. One of the points made in the 2004 *Guardian* article is that neeters seem to have created a subculture where detachment from society is "cool"

---

10 Please see: http://www.guardian.co.uk/education/2004/nov/02/furthereducation.uk, accessed December 27, 2013.

and nothing to be ashamed of. On the contrary, it is easy to get the impression that neeters respond to the lack of opportunities to get into the economy with making a virtue out of having as few strings attached to "society" as possible.

A recent report by the International Labor Organization (ILO) reinforces this image of neeters as a cultural trap for young, unemployed, disenfranchised citizens.[11] After confirming the long-term, alarming upward trend in youth unemployment the report makes an important observation:

> *The youth unemployment crisis in advanced economies is also reflected in longer job search periods and lower job quality. In the majority of OECD countries, one-third or more of young jobseekers are unemployed for at least 6 months. In Europe, an increasing proportion of employed youth are involved in non-standard jobs, including temporary employment and part-time work, and evidence shows that a significant part of the increase is involuntary rather than by choice. Youth part-time employment as a share of total youth employment in Europe was 25.0 per cent in 2011. Another 40.5 per cent of employed youth in the region worked on temporary contracts.*

In other words, at least two out of three citizens aged 25 or younger have only a casual attachment to the labor market. In countries like Greece, Spain and Croatia (which is on the threshold of becoming an EU member) practically no young citizen has anything more than a weak, casual attachment to the job market.

This is an alarming situation. In addition to the enormous political risks of emerging support for radical-solutions movements (think Germany during the Great Depression) there is a very high economic price to be paid for this. As mentioned earlier, these young men and women are the ones who are supposed to inherit society and its economy. They are the ones who, according to the prevailing doctrine of a welfare state, are supposed to pay taxes and fund entitlements while their parents' generation transitions into retirement.

It is easy to understand that this young generation will be attracted by a neeter-style subculture. A lifestyle entirely outside of society as we know it takes on a beauty of its own.

---

11 Please see: http://www.ilo.org/wcmsp5/groups/public/---dgreports/---dcomm/documents/ publication/wcms_212899.pdf, accessed February 3, 2014.

Once a subculture like this has reached large segments of young Europeans, it will be difficult to overcome it. But even if the job-market outlook would get better, the masses of unemployed young, neeters or not, will have lost considerable skills sets and find that they have an education that is either very rusty or out of date for the jobs available.

All this can be overcome, but the cost is significant in terms of, for example, employers investing in their newly hired. The longer mass youth unemployment prevails in Europe, the more the continent will lose in terms of squandered education that won't pay off on the labor market; re-connection costs for the long-term unemployed; lost production time and productivity due to a less-prepared generation trying to take over where others leave off.

Again: large youth unemployment contributes to bringing an economy closer to the shadow realm of industrial poverty.

Then there is the other cost, that which Germany paid after the Weimar Republic. The beauty of the neeeter lifestyle does not last forever. It is fair to assume that neeters for the most part live on welfare or unemployment benefits, systems that are targeted for spending cuts under austerity.

At some point, even mellow young Europeans can turn into political dynamite.

Variable 4: Oversize Government

So far we have blamed big government, or more to the point the welfare state, for being at the eye of the crisis storm, but we have not discussed government in any detail. It is time to fill that gap now, and to begin with we stipulate three premises for why government is not just in the way of a recovery, but contributing to the depth and length of the crisis:

1.   Europe's welfare states impose unbearable tax burdens on the private sector, thus stifling job growth, productivity gains and industrial rejuvenation.

The point about taxes weighing down on the private sector is a common-sense observation with solid back-up in large quantities of literature. It is therefore not something that needs to be argued in any detail.

The one term that needs a bit of a comment is "industrial rejuvenation." We will expand on it below.

2.   Big entitlement programs, the hallmark of the welfare state, discourage workforce participation and turn more people into net consumers of government, as opposed to net contributors.

When people get their basic needs covered by work-free income they prefer leisure to work to a larger extent than if they have to work to feed themselves all the way. As a result workforce participation—or labor supply—declines. This reduction in the supply of labor is part of the reason why GDP grows more slowly. It also explains why private consumption slacks off.

The reduction in workforce participation is symptomatic of the "early" stage of a welfare state. During more "mature" stages of the welfare state workforce participation increases again. The reason for this is not that people can suddenly build a higher standard of living by working more. Instead, as we noted earlier, the explanation is that very high taxes eat in to net earnings of large segments of the workforce. To this we add that long periods of slow GDP growth will slow down the growth in average household earnings. The combination of this and high taxes will simply force people to work more to maintain their standard of living.

It is worth noting that the dependency on entitlements is destructively high both at the early and the mature stages of the welfare state.

3.   When government spending exceeds 40 percent of GDP, the economy is pushed over the edge into industrial poverty.

The rest of this section explains why this is so.

We have already established that when private consumption in a country grows at less than 2 percent per year over a sustained period of time, then that country fulfills one criterion for being in industrial poverty. We have also established that there is a correlation between slow growth in private consumption and a refocusing of the economy away from consumption. In many modern European welfare states, private consumption accounts for about half of GDP. This means that less than half of all the work that people do in those countries goes toward satisfying the needs of their fellow citizens.

What we have not yet established is that there is a correlation between stagnant private consumption and big government. Therefore, Figure 3.4 reports data from 15 industrialized countries, over 15 years, comparing:

- government spending as share of GDP (black dots with red numbers); to

- inflation-adjusted growth rates for private consumption (columns with black numbers).

The data from the 15 countries over the period 1995–2009 is sorted by the size of government. There are 225 observations, each one of which represents one country in one year. Every other decile has 23 observation, every other has 22 observations.

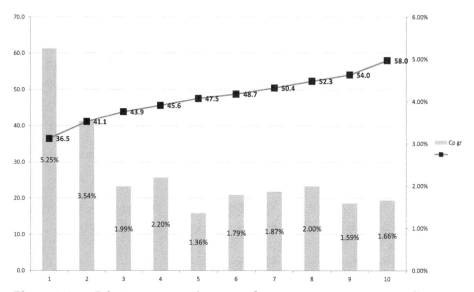

Figure 3.4   Private consumption growth versus government spending
Source: Eurostat, www.ec.europa.eu/eurostat.

In the first decile we have the first 23 observations. Those observations say that when private consumption growth is on average 5.3 percent per year, then the same economy has a government that, on average, spends 36.5 percent of GDP.

Two examples of actual observations from the first decile:

- Ireland, 1996: private consumption growth 7.6 percent, government spending 38.7 percent of GDP;

- United Kingdom, 2000: private consumption growth 4.5 percent, government spending 39 percent of GDP.

The second decile contains the next 22 observations. An example:

- Portugal, 1997: consumption growth 4.4 percent, government spending 41.1 percent of GDP.

The first and second deciles are the only ones where consumption grows significantly faster than 2 percent per year. Once we get to the third decile, we have a government that spends, on average, more than 42 percent of GDP. We also have average growth rates for private consumption that in all observations except one fall short of 2 percent.

Strictly speaking, the data reported in Figure 3.4 *does not prove* that big government causes industrial poverty. However, it gives us good reasons to believe that a country with a big welfare state is strongly at risk of becoming industrially poor. We also have good reasons to put the "tipping point" for the size of government spending at or slightly above 40 percent of GDP.

With this qualification in mind, data from Eurostat shows that as far as big government goes, Europe has already slid deeply into the realm of industrial poverty. Table 3.3 expands the number of observed countries beyond the group of 15 reported in Figure 3.4. It shows the average government spending-to-GDP ratio for all EU member states plus Norway (our highlighted group of 15 states is marked in bold).

Table 3.3   Exports and consumption as share of GDP, 15 countries,
               40 years

Average 2000–10			
Denmark	54.1	Norway	43.6
Sweden	53.8	Czech Republic	43.6
France	53.5	Poland	43.6
Austria	51.0	Malta	42.5
Finland	50.3	Cyprus	42.1
Belgium	50.3	Slovakia	40.4
Hungary	49.9	Luxembourg	40.4
Italy	48.3	Spain	40.4
Greece	47.3	Ireland	38.9
Netherlands	46.7	Bulgaria	38.8
Germany	46.5	Latvia	37.8
Slovenia	46.2	Romania	36.8
Portugal	45.5	Estonia	36.6
United Kingdom	44.1	Lithuania	36.6

Source: Eurostat.

Government spending has not always been at this level. The modern
welfare state emerged after World War II, with the latter half of the
20th century seeing a historically unprecedented expansion of government.
This expansion, led by the world's industrialized nations, was driven by the
desire to build elaborate entitlement programs for both the poor and the
middle class.

    In order to pay for these welfare states, governments of the world's most
advanced nations had to raise taxes. And raise taxes they did. Figure 3.5
illustrates the long-term upward trend in taxes in 23 selected OECD countries.[12]
The largest increase took place in Spain, where the taxes-to-GDP rate went up
2.43 times, or by 243 percent, from 1965 to 2005.

It is beyond question that this global rise in taxes eventually had to take a toll
on the world economy. It is also rather obvious that so long as taxes remain as
high as they are today the outlook for a good, strong recovery is not very good
at all.

---

12 Source: Eurostat. The selection of countries is based on data availability.

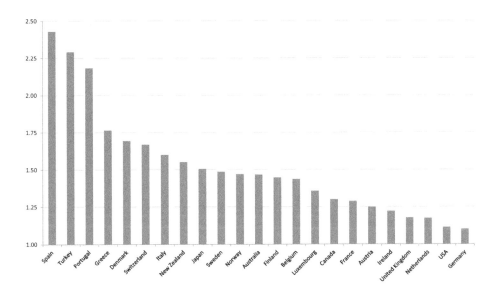

Figure 3.5   Changes in tax-to-GDP ratio
Source: Eurostat, www.ec.europa.eu/eurostat.

In addition to driving up taxes, the construction and expansion of the welfare state has driven up government debts. Despite the fact that the world's welfare states are consuming historically unprecedented levels of their citizens' money, government budgets still run in the red.

This is a very important observation. As we explained earlier, government debt is a major culprit behind the depth and duration of the current economic crisis. In the 15 countries that we pay special attention to, the growth rates in government debt during the crisis have for the most part been eye-popping (see Table 3.4).

Table 3.4   **Growth rates in government debt during the crisis**

	2007	2012
Belgium	84.0%	99.8%
Denmark	27.1%	45.6%
Germany	65.2%	81.9%
Ireland	25.1%	117.6%
Greece	107.2%	156.9%
Spain	36.3%	84.2%
France	64.2%	90.2%
Italy	103.3%	127.0%
Netherlands	45.3%	71.2%
Austria	60.2%	73.2%
Portugal	68.4%	123.7%
Finland	35.2%	53.0%
Sweden	39.4%	38.7%
U.K.	41.3%	89.4%

Source: Eurostat. In this dataset Norway does not report a debt.

Together with the growth rates in taxation reported in Figure 3.5, these numbers reveal a relentless growth in the size of government, not just during the recession but over many decades.

Not surprisingly, government is wasteful. Just the very set-up of government is a recipe for waste: if you get your revenue through forceful action and you have no competition in what you do, how likely is it that you will actually try to use every dollar as efficiently as possible? One of the great benefits of the free-market economy is that anyone who wants to stay in business will have to start with using his resources as efficiently as possible.

One of the best research papers in this area is actually from three economists at the European Central Bank. In 2003 the trio Afonso, Schuknecht and Tanzi published their work under the somewhat uninspiring title *Public Sector Performance: An International Comparison*. They confirm that the bigger government gets, the more it wastes of taxpayers' money (emphasis added):[13]

> *We find that the difference in overall performance is moderate across the sample countries. Countries with "small" public sectors on average*

---

13 Afonso, A., Schuknecht, L. and Tanzi, V., *Public Sector Performance: An International Comparison*, ECB Working Paper 242, July 2003.

report the highest scores for overall performance, and especially for administrative and economic performance. Countries with large public sectors show more equal income distribution. Some countries managed to deliver a significant relative improvement in public sector performance over the last decade (notably, Greece, Portugal, Spain and Ireland). Regarding public sector efficiency, countries with small public sectors report significantly higher indicators than countries with medium-sized or big public sectors. Overall efficiency is highest in Japan, Luxembourg, Australia, the United States and Switzerland. The results of the FDH analysis suggest that "average inefficiency" is about 20%.

Based on their results we can plot how much taxpayers get back from government in the form of services and entitlements on one dollar of taxes (see Figure 3.6).

The three countries at the far right end of the scale were, at the time (2003), also three of the most heavily taxed economies in the world. By contrast, Japan, Luxembourg, the United States and Australia were all low-tax jurisdictions by comparison.

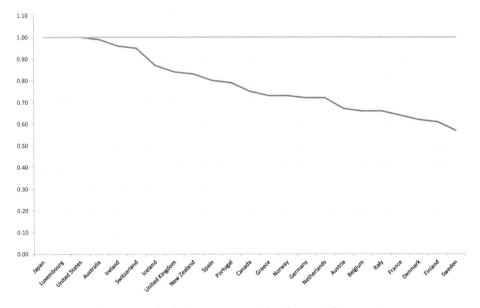

Figure 3.6   How much do taxpayers get back on $1 in taxes?

Source: ECB Working Paper 242; http://www.ecb.int/pub/pdf/scpwps/ecbwp242.pdf.

Not much has changed over the past 10 years when it comes to the relative ranking of these countries. Therefore, even though the results are a decade old by now, they are still valid. The larger government gets, the more of what we put into it gets wasted.

During periods of austerity this waste becomes even more of a problem. To see why, consider the following example.

In year 1 we pay $1,000 in taxes to fund $1,000 worth of government services and entitlements. Assuming a waste of 25 percent as defined by the ECB study, we only get $750 worth of "government" back for our tax dollars. Taxes worth $250 go up in smoke.

Before we proceed, we should note that the $250 worth of taxes that government wastes would have become actual economic activity had government allowed the private sector to keep it. The bigger government gets, the more it wastes simply by continuing to tax and spend.

When this waste is combined with austerity, things get really bad.

In year 2 a recession strikes. Government loses 10 percent of its tax revenues, taking in only $900. At the same time, demand for entitlements force up spending by 10 percent. Government spends $200 on top of the $900, all of it with the same 25 percent waste factor. Nominally, government spending is worth $1,100, but adjusted for waste it amounts to $825.

In year 3 government puts an austerity package to work to eliminate the $200 budget deficit. Spending is cut by that amount. The net-waste value of government spending is now 75 percent of $900, or $675.

It is important to note that taxpayers still pay the same taxes in year 3 as they did in year 1. The only reason why tax revenues are 10 percent lower in year 3 is that some taxpayers are unemployed. In other words, *to the individual taxpayer* government still costs as much as it did before, but he is now getting less money back for his taxes. He is still paying taxes as if government collected $1,000 per year; to the individual taxpayer, government waste is now 32.5 percent.

At some point, this means that individual citizens have to compensate for the loss of government services. If the spending cuts come in the form of reduced unemployment benefits, they have to set aside more money in their savings accounts as a buffer if they lose their jobs. If the cuts ration health care, they have to set aside more money to buy that health care privately (where legal). Such buffer building takes money away from private consumption, thus reducing the annual growth rate in consumer spending. The average citizen spends more money just to maintain his current standard of living—including making up for what government has promised but is no longer providing.

The bigger the waste factor, the stronger is the depressing combination of waste and austerity.

But are not austerity-driven spending cuts supposed to reduce waste and inefficiencies in government bureaucracies?

In theory, yes. But in practice an austerity package is a panic reaction to a budget deficit, a legislative quick-fix aimed at balancing the budget without having to make structural reforms to spending programs. In order to reduce or eliminate government inefficiencies and waste a legislature must pass a structural reform program. While desirable, such reforms practically always take much more time than lawmakers have when they want to just close a budget gap.

The bottom line, then, is that the bigger government grows, the more of a burden government becomes in the form of a wasteful collector of taxpayers' money. Big government and austerity is a bad combination, and a major cause of industrial poverty in Europe.

Industrial Poverty: A Summary

To sum up, a country is in a state of industrial poverty if, for an extended period of time:

1. the inflation-adjusted growth rate in private consumption falls short of 2 percent per year;

2. private consumption falls below 50 percent of GDP;

3. at least one-fifth of the young workforce is unemployed; and

4. government spending or taxes exceed 40 percent of GDP.

As the data reported in this chapter shows, many European countries are in the vicinity of industrial poverty. The main point with the data reported is however not to strictly classify individual countries, but to explain how we can use data for the four variables to analyze industrial poverty.

However, we do have one country, namely Sweden, for which we have presented comprehensive data, enough to allow us to assess where it is with reference to industrial poverty. Based on our analysis in Chapter 2 we can draw the following conclusion:

1.   The actual, inflation-adjusted growth rate in private consumption averages more than 2 percent for a sustained period of time. However, if we adjust the growth rate for the growth in household debt the average rate over time falls well below 2 percent. Debt-funded consumption is nothing more than reversed saving, as the debt must be paid off at some point. Therefore, it reasonable to adjust consumption numbers for how much households borrow.

2.   Private consumption is below 50 percent of GDP.

3.   The latest youth unemployment figure for Sweden indicates that more than one in four young Swedes have no job to go to, nor any other place in society. This deteriorates their work skills and opens up the possibility that they will become net consumers of government entitlements as opposed to net funders. Youth unemployment above 20 percent over a sustained period of time de facto makes it impossible for the economy to operate at a traditional level of full employment. The Swedish youth unemployment rate is well above 20 percent at this point but has not been there for a period long enough to qualify the country as industrially poor.

4.   There is no doubt that Sweden's big government makes Sweden industrially poor.

Now: has Europe today entered a state of industrial poverty? More importantly, how widespread is austerity and what is the potential that industrial poverty rides into Europe's capitals on the backs of austerity? Furthermore: is there another austerity strategy that could avert the problems associated with today's European brand of austerity?

The next chapter answers the first two questions, while a later chapter answers the last question.

Chapter 4a

Europe in 2012:
Entering the Economic Wasteland

In this chapter and the next, Chapter 4b, we will take a close look at what happened on the ground in Europe during the critical crisis year of 2012. During that year the crisis reached a critical mass. It also collided with the full force of austerity policies. As is evident in experiences from individual EU member states, the outcome was that Europe entered an economic wasteland where the continent may find itself stuck for decades to come.

Chapter 4a visits the three worst-hit countries, Greece, Spain and Italy. Chapter 4b continues the trip through several other EU states, showing that the crisis was not limited to the Mediterranean rim.

Bad Forecasting, Bad Policies, Bad Consequences

Ambrose Evans-Pritchard is a renowned, high-quality British journalist. Currently he holds the position of international business editor at the *Daily Telegraph*. He has three decades under his belt covering world politics and economic policy from three continents and writes with a sharp and eloquent pen.

On December 9, 2012, Evans-Pritchard sounded the alarm about what was happening in Europe as a result of the barrage of austerity that Brussels was directing toward troubled EU member states:[1]

> *Like the generals of the First World War, Europe's leaders seem determined to send wave after wave of their youth into the barbed wire of tight money, bank deleveraging, and fiscal austerity a l'outrance.*

---

[1] Evans-Pritchard, A., "Europe clings to scorched-earth ideology as depression deepens," *Daily Telegraph*, December 9, 2012. Available at: http://www.telegraph.co.uk/finance/comment/ambroseevans_pritchard/9733486/Europe-clings-to-scorched-earth-ideology-as-depression-deepens.html, accessed December 27, 2013.

> *The strategy of triple-barrelled contraction across a string of inter-linked countries has been the greatest policy debacle since the early 1930s. The outcome over the last three years has been worse than forecast at every stage, and in every key respect.*

His point about the lack of forecasting success is important. Nobody forecasted the crisis. Beyond that, Evans-Pritchard takes a refreshingly sincere approach to Europe as she stood in late 2012:

> *The eurozone has crashed back into double-dip recession. It will contract a further 0.3pc next year, according to a chastened European Central Bank. The ECB omitted mention of its own role in this fiasco by allowing all key measures of the money supply to stall in mid-2012, with the time-honoured consequences six months to a year later. The North has been engulfed at last by the contractionary holocaust it imposed on the South. French car sales crashed 19pc [November 2012], even before its fiscal shock therapy – 2pc of GDP next year.*

Other countries hit hard are Germany, for which spring 2013 forecasts predict complete economic stagnation,[2] and the Netherlands, which was thrown into an untimely election due to austerity measures in the spring of 2012. In fact, if the entire euro-zone would see even a penny's worth of growth in 2013, it would be cause for celebration.

Evans-Pritchard goes on to paint a thoroughly depressing, yet painfully accurate, picture of Europe as of December 2012:

> *The youth jobless rate has reached 58pc in Greece, 55.8pc in Spain, 39.1pc in Portugal, 36.5pc in Italy, 30.1pc in Slovakia, and 25.5pc in France, with all the known damage this does to the life-trajectory of the victims and the productive dynamism of these economies ... The labour share of total income has fallen to a 60-year low, eating away at demand. This is a formula for perma-slump.*

The effects of youth unemployment are devastating, economically as well as socially and culturally. When such large segments of the growing generation are barred from carving out a start to their adult life; when they are perpetually unable to build a career, let alone find a job; when there is no way for them to

---

2   See Eurostat Quarterly National Accounts Statistics. Available at: http://epp.eurostat.ec.europa. eu/portal/page/portal/national_accounts/introduction, accessed December 27, 2013.

build character by supporting themselves; they will never be ready or willing to inherit society. Very few of them will rise to replace the leaders of the older generation.

They will turn their backs on what their parents are leaving for them. This will have formidable consequences down the road, but one of the most immediate effects will be that economic stagnation will be perpetuated.

In addition to the disenfranchisement of the young, the crisis brings stagnant earnings to the majority of the workforce. This has a direct effect on private spending, which in turn has a major dampening effect on the economy. This reinforces the stagnation in Europe and sinks the continent even deeper into the macroeconomic quagmire.

When the economy stagnates, so does the tax base. When, in turn, half and more of all young people are unable to find jobs, and when large segments of older workers are also unemployed, the costs of the welfare state to taxpayers continues to increase. This puts more and more pressure on the government budget and opens up a deficit.

At this point, Europe's political leaders panicked. The Commissioners of the European Union—the de facto cabinet of the EU—joined forces with the European Central Bank and started demanding of member states that they balance their budgets immediately. National political leaders in Greece, Ireland, Italy, Spain and Portugal all agreed.

They all launched varying versions of austerity packages—higher taxes, less spending—in the hope that it would allow them to close the budget gap.

But there was also a secondary purpose behind austerity. If all that mattered was to close a budget gap, then Europe's governments could easily have simply shut down a few entitlement programs. The social cost aside, it would have been a simple matter from a strict accounting viewpoint. But they chose not to do that. Instead they chose spending cuts that reduced the percentage of income covered by unemployment benefits; they raised taxes to ease the burden of spending cuts on the entitlement programs in their welfare state.

Even if they had put all the budget adjustments on the spending side, the goal would still have been to preserve the welfare state—just a bit smaller than before. This is a crucial element in Europe's unfolding tragedy. The balanced budget gets more attention in Europe than in the United States.

It has constitutional status in the EU: in 1992, when the EU constitution was ratified as the Maastricht Treaty (later Lisbon Treaty), Article 104c dictated that no member state could have a budget deficit that exceeded 3 percent of the country's GDP.

While strictly speaking not a balanced-budget requirement, this article has taken the form in EU policy of a requirement on member states to not run deficits at all. This has been especially obvious during the current crisis. Member states have focused all their fiscal policy on trying to balance their government budgets.

American fiscal hawks may applaud this, pointing to the enormous federal deficit. There is a strong rhetorical connection between fiscal hawkishness and arguments for austerity to be brought to the United States. However, in order to find the best way to bring U.S. government finances into good order, and to structurally and permanently reduce the size of government in a sustainable way, it is important that we get an in-depth understanding of what austerity has meant to Europe.

As the Europeans define austerity, government combines tax increases and spending cuts into a package aimed at reducing a budget deficit. While there has been some debate over which combination of the two is less harmful to the economy, Europe has not yet found a combination that won't lead to stalled GDP growth, high and rising unemployment and persistent budget deficits:

- tax increases do not work because they drain the private sector of money it desperately needs in a recession;

- spending cuts have proven to have more of a negative effect on economic activity during this recession than economists had generally thought.[3]

Sweden was able to close its budget deficit only by permanently excluding 7 percent of the workforce from the opportunity to support themselves.

Since the purpose of austerity is to reduce a budget deficit, the policy strategy relies on transferring money from the private sector to government. This happens even if austerity relies entirely on spending cuts. Here is why.

---

3   Blanchard, O. and Leigh, D., *Growth Forecast Errors and Fiscal Multipliers*, Working Paper 1301, International Monetary Fund, Washington, DC, January 2013.

Suppose government spends $1,000 per year and takes in $1,000 in taxes. A recession hits and some people lose their jobs. They go from being taxpayers to collecting unemployment benefits. Spending now goes up to $1,100 while tax revenues fall to $900. We have a $200 budget deficit.

Along comes austerity. Suppose lawmakers raise taxes by $200. Taxes must go up by more than 20 percent, since we have fewer taxpayers now than before the recession. The effective meaning of this is that the price of government-provided services has increased. Taxpayers get exactly the same package from government as they did when taxes were lower.

The only net effect is that the private sector has less money to spend.

Suppose now that instead of raising taxes, lawmakers cut spending by $200. This money currently pays for services such as education, law enforcement and cash entitlements to the unemployed. Cuts in services will either lay off workers or reduce the quality of the services provided. When people get laid off they go from being income earners to living on unemployment benefits. (Remember that this is happening in a recession, so the prospect of laid-off government workers finding a private-sector job is not very good.)

As they go from earning a paycheck to taking entitlements they cost government less money, but they also do not pay income taxes. But we must also acknowledge that taxpayers are getting an inferior product from government than they did before: there are fewer teachers in the schools and fewer police officers on the streets, yet taxpayers are paying the same amount of money for those services.

In order to protect their children from the deteriorating quality of public schools, parents with money available will buy private-school services instead. To do this they have to take money from current spending—their taxes are the same as before—which leads the private sector to shift what it is producing from complementing government into compensating for it.

In essence: parents are paying twice for their children's education, sharply raising the cost of education to society.

Suppose instead that the spending cuts are aimed at entitlements, such as unemployment benefits. This will not affect taxpayers directly as they are not receiving unemployment checks. However, indirectly they will be affected. The unemployed have less money to spend which reduces spending in, for example, supermarkets and discount stores. On top of that, taxpayers realize that if they lose their jobs they will have even less to live on after the cut in benefits. As a result they will reduce some of their current spending and shore up savings instead.

A cut in government spending, which negatively affects GDP, is accompanied by a reduction in private-sector spending. The recession worsens, government gets less tax revenue and the deficit remains.

A Note on Government Waste

There is an argument to be made that government is wasteful and that spending cuts in a recession is a good time to reduce that waste. By reducing waste, we would avoid the negative effects mentioned above and in fact give taxpayers a better bundle of products for their taxes.

Only a full-scale socialist would deny that government is wasteful. In theory the argument about reducing waste is correct, and the recession would indeed be a good time to get rid of waste. However, as with so much else in economics there is quite a distance between theory and reality here.

To begin with, "waste" is a vague term that has different meanings depending on where in government we look. The waste going on in the administrative offices of the federal government around the National Mall in Washington, DC, is probably very different from the waste you might find among the 60 men and women that constitute Alaska's total force of state troopers. When we talk about government waste, do we mean inefficiencies as when the IRS takes a lot of time to review an application from an organization for 501(c)(3) status, or do we mean the extra money that army colonels and generals spend on furnishing their offices with higher-quality desks and chairs?

Most of us would say "all of the above," and there is nothing wrong with that. Every function of an organization, including government, must function as efficiently as possible. But waste of the kinds mentioned above is not something we can get rid of by pushing the "flush" button during a recession. Waste is more often than not a structural problem, built in to the very organization itself. Getting rid of it takes more time than we have during a recession.

Another side of the waste problem is that it sometimes overlaps with the question of what the essential functions of government actually are. It is easy to argue that public education is not an essential government function, but that does not mean that all of what goes on inside our public schools is waste. There is good evidence that public education costs more and provides poorer results than private education,[4] indicating that government is wasteful when it provides education for our children. But how would we bring public-school spending and results on par with the private sector during a recession?

The only really effective tool is to cut appropriations to a per-student level comparable to private alternatives. However, that presumes that private and public education are similarly organized, or that public schools are able to adjust their organization and educational policy to those of private schools. That may be true, but a far better way to find out is to structurally change the way we provide education for our children—namely to transition from today's publicly dominated system to an entirely private model.

Privatization solves the waste problem permanently, and is therefore the preferable remedy for waste in government. There is only so much we can do in terms of reducing the cost of government through waste reduction; what do we do in the next recession when the waste is out of the system?

In a later section we will return to government waste and inefficiency. There is research that shows a clear and compelling correlation between the size of government and its level of inefficiency: the bigger government gets, the less efficient it is. This tells us that we have a lot to gain from reducing the size of government, but it also tells us that the elimination of waste and inefficiencies in government is very much a structural phenomenon that comes with the very existence of government.

A hunt for waste and inefficiencies in a recession easily translates into simple spending cuts. This does not guarantee that the inefficiencies go away. If a school district cuts funding for its schools, whose interests are the school board officials, school administrators and teachers' union representatives going to look after?

---

4   A classic study by the World Bank: "Public schools – and private; which are more efficient?" *World Bank Policy Research Bulletin*, Vol. 3, Number 1, January 1992. A 1997 report by the Mackinac Center suggested that the cost for public education is higher than officially reported: http://www.mackinac.org/article.aspx?ID=1118, accessed December 27, 2013. In 2010 the Cato Institute followed up with a report to confirm these findings: http://www.cato.org/publications/policy-analysis/they-spend-what-real-cost-public-schools, accessed December 27, 2013. A counterpoint: http://schoolfinance101.wordpress.com/2010/02/20/stossel-coulson-misinformation-on-private-vs-public-school-costs/, accessed December 27, 2013.

It is better to tackle the waste issue at a structural level and not as a means to balance the government budget in a recession.

Austerity on the Ground

The larger government gets, the more its taxes weigh down the economy. Big government spending in turn crowds out private-sector activity; together the two frontlines of big government discourage workforce participation, stifle growth and reduce consumption and investments relative to what we can see in small-government economies.[5]

As the economy slows down under big government, it becomes increasingly difficult for the welfare state to fund all its entitlement programs. Tax revenues no longer grow on par with the citizens' demand for entitlements. Slow growth keeps more people in low incomes, making more people eligible for money from the welfare state; in order to pay for the entitlements the welfare state needs more tax revenues. Those revenues won't come from stronger growth, so the only way out is to raise taxes.

If the trend upward in taxes is slow and the growth in entitlement spending is slow, the welfare state's negative effect on the private sector will not seem to be dramatic. However, as the erosion of growth and private-sector employment and investment continues, the economy eventually becomes so fragile that it only takes a regular recession for the welfare state to open up a huge budget deficit.

That is exactly what happened in Greece. What started out as a financial crisis, small enough for the world's banking system to absorb the shock, rapidly grew to a major deficit crisis as welfare states could no longer keep their budgets in check. Not even drastic austerity measures, with harsh cuts to benefits and punitive tax increases, could save Greece, Spain, Portugal or Italy.

Eventually, Greece, Italy and Spain came to a point where they were having problems making payments on their debts. This turned their Treasury bonds into high-risk assets on the balance sheets of Europe's banks—and all of a sudden the containable bank crisis spiraled out of control.

---

5   Larson, S.R., "The economic case for limited government," *Prosperitas*, Vol. VII, Issue III; April 2007, Center for Freedom and Prosperity. Available at: http://archive.freedomandprosperity. org/Papers/rahncurve/rahncurve.pdf, accessed December 27, 2013.

Politicians panicked. They saw government and banks bleeding money. Their gut reaction was to try to plug the hole in the government budgets by means of more austerity. Things went from bad to worse, and as of the spring of 2013 the crisis is so bad that even otherwise modest voices are now reverberating with fear.

Fear for Europe's future.

A good example is the highly respected think tank the Breugel Forum. Based in Brussels, Belgium, the Breugel Forum is an influential voice in European public policy. Usually its publications speak with a measured voice and refrain from bold language. However, in a report released in April, 2013 its tone has changed notably. Here is its summary of Europe's present situation:[6]

> *Europe's pre-crisis growth performance was disappointing enough, but the performance since the onset of the crisis has been even more dismal ... while total output of the EU15 countries (EU members before 2004) exceeded that of the United States by 15 percent in 1982, it is expected to be 17 percent lower in 2017 ... Unlike the U.S. and Japan, Europe's growth and unemployment numbers have consistently disappointed since 2007.*

Then it notes (emphasis added):

> *Productivity developments remain weak, even in EU countries with healthier private and public balance sheets. Unemployment continues to grow and set new records. This is again in contrast to the developments in the U.S., where the initial impact of the recession on employment was much worse, but where job creation has resumed.*

Its point about private and public balance sheets is very important. What the Breugel Forum is saying is that both countries with big and small government debt and with big and small government deficits are suffering from sluggish or no growth, high unemployment and a very dismal outlook on the future.

In short: the focus on trying to balance government budgets has at the very best made no difference. But that is a generous interpretation of what

---

6   Darvas, Z., Pisani-Ferry, J. and Wolff, G.B., "Europe's growth problem (and what to do about it)," Parliamentary testimony, Bruegel Institute, April 12, 2013. Available at: http://www.bruegel.org/publications/publication-detail/publication/776-europes-growth-problem-and-what-to-do-about-it/, accessed December 27, 2013.

happened during 2012; a more realistic conclusion is that those countries that actively tried to balance their government budget during the recession have ended up in a far worse position than otherwise.

Here are some examples.

Greece

Table 4.1   Greece

	2009	2010	2011	2012	2013	2014
Private consumption growth	2.0	1.9	1.4	0.4	-1.2	-0.4
Youth unemployment	25.7	32.8	44.4	55.3	—	—
Consumption share of GDP	71.8	70.7	70.1	68.1	—	—
Taxes to GDP	38.3	40.6	42.4	44.7	—	—

Source: Eurostat.

The large consumption-to-GDP share in the Greek economy indicates that the government would not have to do a whole lot to initiate a private-sector driven recovery. Greeks spend about as much of their GDP on private consumption as Americans do, though that is gradually changing for the worse. The decline in the consumption growth rate combined with the destructive increase in the tax-to-GDP rate will thwart any attempts by the private sector to restore the Greek economy to where it was before the Great Big Austerity Campaign began.

It is rare to see such sharp increases in taxation over such a short period of time as in Greece. This alone should have sent economists and politicians in Athens scrambling for alternatives to austerity. Not many did, but as a July 2012 story from Yahoo News reported, there were exceptions:[7]

> *Greece's new government will present "alarming" data on its recession and unemployment to international debt inspectors this week, in a bid to renegotiate the terms of its bailout agreements. Spokesman Simos Kedikoglou said in a television interview Tuesday that the data would demonstrate that the current austerity program was counterproductive.*

---

7   "Greece to present debt inspectors 'alarming' data," AP-Yahoo News, July 3, 2012. Available at: http://news.yahoo.com/greece-present-debt-inspectors-alarming-data-095944151--finance. html, accessed December 27, 2013.

Greece had at the time been through years of painful austerity programs in exchange for cash from the ECB and the IMF to continue funding its welfare state. Yahoo News again:

> *Greece is relying on rescue loans from its partners in the eurozone and the International Monetary Fund to avoid bankruptcy. In exchange, it has made painful austerity cuts, such as tax hikes and cuts to public sector jobs, pensions and salaries. Along with uncertainty over the country's finances, those austerity measures have hit the economy hard — it is in a fifth year of recession, with unemployment topping 22 percent, roughly double the eurozone average. The Greek government will argue that it cannot withstand the current pace of austerity terms.*

That unemployment number is from the summer of 2012. It has increased by one-third since then—in just one year. That is an alarming rise in joblessness, as alarming as the fact that the Greek economy has shrunk by 25 percent during five years of austerity bombardment (see Figure 4.1).

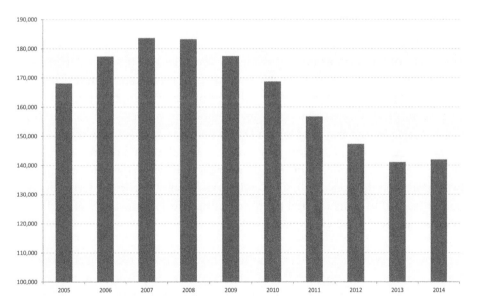

Figure 4.1   Greece GDP, fixed prices
Source: Eurostat.

This is a virtual collapse of a modern, industrialized economy, with opportunities and ambitions of people, especially the young, being wiped out in droves.

Under such conditions there comes a point when a country becomes ungovernable. However, as a report by the *EUobserver* on August 2, 2012, explained, there was no attempt in Athens to connect the economic disaster unfolding before the very eyes of the legislators to the political radicalization of their country. To the incumbent prime minister and his majority, it was—for lack of better words—crisis as usual:[8]

> *Coalition partners in Greece have so far failed to agree the details of €11.5 billion worth of spending cuts required by international lenders to unblock more aid, just as a minister warned cash reserves are drying up. The three-party coalition led by Conservative Prime Minister Antonis Samaras was set to meet again on [August 1] and try to reach an agreement, after failing to do so in the past few days. Samaras had given reassurances to the troika of international lenders (the EU commission, the International Monetary Fund and European Central Bank) ... that the cuts will be laid out in detail by next week, Ekathimerini newspaper reports.*

The leader of the socialist party, Evangelos Venizelos, protested and expressed fear that more cuts could exacerbate an already fragile social and economic situation. His protest was not at all without merit. In the June election 39 percent of all Greeks voted for anti-democratic parties such as the Hugo Chavez-style Syriza and the Golden Dawn neo-Nazis. This made the majority behind the governing coalition very fragile, a fact that put enormous pressure on the Greek government. The anti-democratic extremists have done their best to capitalize on the crisis, with Golden Dawn showing particular fortitude. It is not far-fetched to conclude that the devastating effects of austerity played right into the hands of those extremists.

However, as the *EUobserver* reported, this was not something that the EU seemed to be particularly worried about. It continued to put enormous pressure on the Greek government to carry on with one destructive austerity measure after another:

> *EU commission chief Jose Manuel Barroso, during a visit to the country [in July 2012], told Samaras in front of reporters that "words are not*

---

8   Please see: http://euobserver.com/19/117113, accessed December 27, 2013.

enough" and the only advice he can give is "deliver, deliver, deliver"
on the promises made. Meanwhile, a Greek deputy finance minister on
Tuesday warned there is no time to lose as cash reserves are quickly
drying up in the absence of the next tranche from the €130 billion
bailout agreed in March [2012].

Something would have to give. According to another story from the *EUobserver*
on July 27, 2012, it was not going to be the EU. Its commitment to more austerity
in Greece was unwavering:[9]

Greece must stop only talking about reforms but actually carry them
out before its lenders' trust runs out, EU commission president Jose
Manuel Barroso said on his first visit to the country since it had to
be bailed out. "To maintain the trust of European and international
partners, the delays must end. Words are not enough. Actions are
much more important," he said Thursday evening (25 July) ...
Samaras, for his part, said: "I told Mr Barroso that we are determined
as a government to move ahead with structural changes, privatisation
and implementation of agreed measures." The two also discussed the
need to tackle ... endemic tax evasion, to "drastically reduce" public
expenditure, to change the business climate and better use EU funds
... Newspaper reports, meanwhile, have variously said that it would be
impossible to get a third Greek bailout through parliament and that the
IMF is not prepared to give any more money to the country.

But the same *EUobserver* story also noted that the Greek people were not the
first ones to give up either:

In Greece itself the three-party government has an uphill struggle to
persuade citizens to stomach more austerity. It has tentatively agreed
to see through a €11.5bn package of spending cuts for 2013–14, agreed
months ago but held up due to elections in May and June.

On August 1, 2012, *Russia Today* reported[10] that Golden Dawn was out in the
streets:

---

9   Please see: http://euobserver.com/19/117078, accessed December 27, 2013.
10 "Rescue, nationalist style: Golden Dawn hands out food to Greeks only," *Russia Today*, August
    1, 2012. Available at: http://www.rt.com/news/golden-down-hand-out-food-620/, accessed
    December 27, 2013.

handing out food to Greeks coping with a worsening crisis. The event had a distinct nationalist odor, as people had to prove their citizenship in order to receive goods. Hundreds lined up outside Parliament, where the extreme-right activists were giving away potatoes, pasta, milk and olive oil. According to a Golden Dawn spokesperson, all the products were produced or distributed by local businesses. To obtain food packages, those in line had to present their ID card to validate their citizenship. The ultra-nationalist Golden Dawn, which many say is neo-Nazi, is notorious for constant assaults on immigrants. Last month the party threatened to remove immigrants and their children from hospitals and kindergartens ... Public support for the party has dramatically increased, twenty-fold, since elections in 2009. This May, Golden Dawn gained 7 per cent of the vote at the parliamentary elections, managing to pass the threshold for the first time.

In other words, the economic crisis—really a depression—was driving Greek politics to the extremes. With such a shift, focus on solving the crisis will shift to whatever ideological hardliners prescribe, a fact that can only make matters worse for the Greek people.

By mid-August the *EUobserver* reported that time was running out—the euro-zone countries that were keeping Greece afloat were rapidly losing their patience.[11] Pressured from voters who, tired of austerity, had given anti-democratic voices a strong presence in parliament, the Greek government managed to make its case to the EU. The austerity measures it had already implemented had forced mass lay-offs of public-sector employees, drastically cut welfare spending, slashed unemployment benefits, increased health care rationing and almost wiped out subsidies for pharmaceutical drugs.

At the same time, taxes had remained high and, in some cases, even gone up. This had pushed Greece to the brink of social and political chaos, driven in part by the resurgence of Nazism within the hallways of Greek parliamentary democracy.

The prospect of Nazis once again gaining political influence in a European country was enough to convince Greece's lenders to cut the government some slack:[12]

---

11 Please see: http://euobserver.com/economic/117238, accessed December 27, 2013.
12 Please see: http://euobserver.com/economic/117238, accessed December 27, 2013.

According to internal documents obtained by the Financial Times, the €11.5 billion worth of spending cuts the government is still struggling to cobble together would be spread over four years until 2016, instead of the 2014 deadline that is currently expected by Greece's lenders. In order for the plan to work, Greece would need an extra €20 billion to support the budget as the annual deficit reduction in 2013–2014 would be smaller than planned. But Athens would not seek extra money on top of the €130 billion bailout agreed in March, FT reports, and instead would ask for its repayment of the first bailout it received in 2014 to be postponed until 2020.

Despite somewhat more lenient conditions, one cannot help but draw parallels between this repayment plan and the one forced upon Germany after World War I. At the Treaty of Versailles the winners of the war imposed such extreme repayment conditions on Germany that John Maynard Keynes, the British economist who was present at the negotiations, foresaw the rise of totalitarianism as a direct result. It is easy to see why nationalists can benefit from a situation where the people of a nation are starving yet foreign creditors demand money that could have gone toward feeding the poor.

But it was not just the prospect of a continued rise in political extremism that helped Greece make its case for creditors to be more understanding. The crashing economy was a big enough reason on its own:[13]

In support of his plea, Samaras is likely to invoke the worsening recession – 6.2 percent of GDP according to the latest Eurostat figures published on Tuesday – and its record unemployment rate of over 23 percent. "The deficit reduction demanded for the period 2013–2014 is excessive. An overdose of austerity is self-defeating," said Iannis Mourmouras, the prime minister's chief economic adviser, according to the FT.

Austerity is not only self-defeating in overdose. It is self-defeating by definition. But that was too much even for Greece's government to grasp at this time. They soldiered on, bravely, trying to walk an ever thinner line between the demands from their creditors in the EU and their increasingly desperate citizens.

One solution—a radical one—that was being considered at the time was for Greece to simply leave the currency union. Many voices, including very vocal

---

13 Please see: http://euobserver.com/economic/117238, accessed December 27, 2013.

radicals in the Greek parliament, called for an exit as a fix-it-all solution for the suffering nation.

The fact that a member state of the currency union has come to the point of possible exit is a remarkable turn of events. The euro is little more than a decade old, and it was not more than two decades ago that the members of the European Communities signed the founding document, the Maastricht Treaty (later modified to the Lisbon Treaty). During the years from Maastricht to the euro there was no end to the europhoria. Never in the history of Europe has the future been painted in such rosy colors as it was in the 1990s. The Europeans were promised better-everything: more prosperity, more jobs, better health care, safe and secure retirement benefits, more sunshine …

Today the picture is amazingly different. The EU and the "European project" are reminiscent of RMS *Titanic* in more ways than one: its architects and project leaders vastly overstated its merits, and it has now run into its own iceberg.

The welfare state.

Slowly but steadily, entitlement spending has outgrown tax revenues, especially (but not only) in Greece. Borrowing has caused a drainage on future tax revenues and weighed down on the common currency. Thanks to the fact that Greece shares its currency with Germany, it has in effect been able to borrow on Germany's good credit. That stretched Greece's borrowing way beyond what the country would have been able to do on its own currency.

Greece was perceived as irresponsible by the EU, the ECB, the IMF and Germany. There were whispers in the EU that Greece would be forced to leave the currency union as a result of its highly irresponsible borrowing. That, however, never happened, mostly because the ECB realized that more countries might want to leave voluntarily. On August 20, 2012, the *EUobserver* reported:[14]

> German member of the ECB board, Joerg Asmussen has told Frankfurter
> Rundschau that he prefers Greece to stay in the eurozone but its exit

---

14 Please see: http://euobserver.com/tickers/117282, accessed December 27, 2013. A full interview with Mr. Asmussen was published in *Frankfurter Rundschau* (in German): http://www.fr-online. de/wirtschaft/ezb-direktor-zur-eurokrise-asmussen---griechenland-soll-im-euro-bleiben- ,1472780,16920556,view,asFirstTeaser.html, accessed December 27, 2013.

*would be "manageable". A Greek exit would be "associated with a loss
of growth and higher unemployment and it would be very expensive,"
he said.*

However, the price for Greece to stay in the currency union has been very
high. Austerity is still holding the Greek people in a tight grip, with terrible
consequence. A story from Reuters in June 2012 gave a chilling glimpse of life
in Greece in the midst of the austerity purge:[15]

> *Greece's rundown state hospitals are cutting off vital drugs, limiting
> non-urgent operations and rationing even basic medical materials for
> exhausted doctors as a combination of economic crisis and political
> stalemate strangle health funding. With Greece now in its fifth year
> of deep recession, trapped under Europe's biggest public debt burden
> and dependent on international help to keep paying its bills, the effects
> are starting to bite deeply into vital services. "It's a matter of life
> and death for us," said Persefoni Mitta, head of the Cancer Patients'
> Association, recounting the dozens of calls she gets a day from Greeks
> needing pricey, hard-to-find cancer drugs. "Why are they depriving
> us of life?"*

As part of its austerity policies, the Greek government cut tax-funded subsidies
for medical drugs. As the Reuters story explains, this had some serious
consequences. Pharmaceutical companies, who normally provide discounted
purchasing plans to poor nations, had to start putting together emergency
plans to avoid a catastrophic disruption of the supply of medicines to the
Greek people. While the plans were primarily designed for a Greek secession
from the euro—an economic event that could have downright catastrophic
consequences for the already hard-beaten economy—the drug makers were
also mindful of the dire consequences for the Greek health care system that
followed from "a tangle of unpaid bills."

In other words:

- the Greek government had decided to subsidize medicines as part
  of an effort toward universal health care;

---

15 "Greek health system crumbles under weight of crisis," Reuters, June 14, 2012. Available
    at: http://www.reuters.com/article/2012/06/14/us-greece-health-idUSBRE85D1IO20120614,
    accessed December 27, 2013.

- when the Greek economy collapsed and started its five-year tailspin, the promises of heavy medical drug subsidies turned out to be just one more that the Greek government could not keep;

- because of the sharp rise in taxation (see Table 4.1) the Greek people have less money than ever to pay for medicines out of pocket;

- domestic providers of pharmaceutical products can no longer collect enough cash from their customers (never mind the austerity-minded government) to pay their bills to the businesses that supply the drugs.

The welfare state strikes again, causing heavy rationing of critical pharmaceutical products. More and more pharmacies decline to accept credit as a means of paying for medicine—they, too, have bills to pay and credit defaults are riding in droves on the coat-tails of austerity. Or, as the Reuters story of June 2012 explained:

> Long queues have been forming outside a handful of pharmacies that still provide medication on credit – the rest are demanding cash upfront until the government pays up a subsidy backlog of 762 million euros, or nearly $1 billion. "We're not talking about painkillers here – we've learned to live with physical pain – we need drugs to keep us alive," Mitta, a petite former marathon runner and herself a cancer survivor, said in a voice shaky with emotion.

It is worth noticing that she is not in line for food. Even in the midst of a terrible economic crisis, the free market can still feed the Greek people. And while it kept doing so throughout 2012, the government-dominated health care system was under pressure from the EU, the ECB and the IMF to make even more "big cuts" to the health care system as part of yet another budget-balancing effort.

The big question is how much more austerity a country like Greece can take before it collapses. An August 2012 story in the British newspaper the *Guardian* reported:[16]

---

16 "Greece's health care system is on the brink of catastrophe," *Guardian*, August 5, 2011. Available at: http://www.guardian.co.uk/world/2011/aug/05/greece-healthcare-brink-catastrophe, accessed December 27, 2013.

> *Adonis Kostakos is unemployed and diabetic. Aged 50, he last worked*
> *regularly four years ago in the port of Piraeus. Back then he used Greece's*
> *public hospital system to have his blood sugar checked and get his*
> *medication. These days, receiving no unemployment benefit, he cannot*
> *afford to pay for his drugs or the new €5 hospital fee introduced as part*
> *of Greece's austerity measures. So today Kostakos has come to a free*
> *clinic in the shipbuilding town of Perama, where he lives, to pick up his*
> *medication. The drop-in surgery run by the global charity Médecins du*
> *Monde was originally set up to cater for illegal immigrants. But today,*
> *there are only native Greeks.*

The *Guardian* story also gave a glimpse of how the Greek equivalent to Medicaid
left people in a vacuum:

> *Others come into the clinic. A middle-aged man with swollen legs from*
> *heart disease needs diuretics; a younger man, who once worked in the*
> *nearby shipyards, comes in to be treated for high blood pressure. "When*
> *I came here," says Padakis, "I didn't expect to be treating Greeks.*
> *I had no idea so many Greeks had these problems. I thought I would*
> *be working with illegal immigrants." On a typical day the clinic sees*
> *around 20 people. "The problems are never simple. Sometimes people*
> *don't have the correct insurance or it takes time for the right papers*
> *to come through. Sometimes it is as simple as the fact that they don't*
> *have a few euros for the bus to go to the hospital for an appointment, so*
> *they come here." These people are often new poor … and an additional*
> *problem is that the hospitals are now charging each time someone visits.*

The deterioration of the Greek health care system came together with higher
taxes, which again means that the taxpayers paid more to get less from
government. While different in design and execution, the Greek austerity
policies have a strong resemblance to the Swedish package of 1995–98. Just
as in Sweden, people in Greece have less money to spend on alternatives
to the services that government promised and charged taxes for, but is no
longer delivering. (Not to mention that government never do away with
their monopolies during periods of austerity.) Instead, they find themselves
having to cut down on other expenses in order to pay higher taxes—and go
into debt, as the example with the medical drugs showed.

This depresses the economy further and erodes the tax base even more.
The vicious circle of austerity, government deficits and a perennial recession
continues.

One more glimpse of Greece's crumbling health care system from the same Guardian article:

> *If the clinic in Perama is an example of how bad things have got for those at the bottom of Greece's ruined economy, elsewhere doctors and patients have their own horror stories to tell in a corrupt health system where paying bribes to doctors is commonplace. As a result of the crisis, doctors' wages in the public system have been cut in line with other government workers, while hospitals fear being merged and face regular shortages of materials. Most damaging is how an already unequal health system has become more unequal still – a three-tier affair that discriminates systematically against those most vulnerable and least able to afford health care, marginalising them still further in society.*

It is understandable that the vast majority of Greeks thought that the austerity-driven spending cuts were unfair.[17] This is logical, of course, given that those who depend on the welfare state, and therefore are hit by austerity, are first and foremost the poor and needy.

However, popular dislike of austerity did not prevent yet more of the same. In September 2012 the Greek parliament went ahead and approved yet another round of spending cuts, dictated to them by the EU–ECB–IMF troika. This led to even higher tensions between the Greek government and its voters, taxpayers and entitlement consumers. On September 8, 2012 Reuters reported:[18]

> *Thousands of Greeks marched at an annual fair in Greece's second-biggest city on Saturday to protest against a new round of wage and pension cuts demanded by international lenders in exchange for aid to stave off bankruptcy. The demonstration by about 15,000 trade unionists and leftists was the first major protest against a nearly 12-billion-euro austerity package being readied by Prime Minister Antonis Samaras to appease EU and IMF inspectors who arrived in Athens on Friday to review Greece's reform progress.*

---

17 "Most Greeks feel new austerity measures are unfair – poll," Phantis.com, September 23, 2012. Available at: http://www.phantis.com/news/most-greeks-feel-new-austerity-measures-are-unfair-poll, accessed December 27, 2013.
18 "Thousands of Greeks protest against new round of austerity cuts," Reuters, September 8, 2012. Available at: http://www.reuters.com/article/2012/09/08/greece-protests-idUSL6E8K81C1201 20908, accessed December 27, 2013.

Reuters also noted that the crisis had set off an epidemic of business bankruptcies. With the alarming rates of unemployment among all groups of able-bodied Greeks, this should make every conscientious elected official in Athens reconsider the alleged virtues of austerity. But not the administration led by Prime Minister Samaras. Together with his treasury secretary, Mr. Stournaras, he charged ahead, cheered on by his peers in other EU member states. All Mr. Samaras and Mr. Stournaras did was to try to get a year or two extra to force the latest austerity package on to the shoulders of the Greek people.

According to *Der Spiegel*, on November 6, 2012, this had predictable effects:[19]

> *Thousands of Greeks took to the streets of Athens on Tuesday on the first of two days of strikes to protest yet more biting austerity measures. Their anger is palpable, but if parliament fails to pass the cuts on Wednesday, the consequences could be dire.*

At that time, Greece was nearing the end of its fifth straight year with shrinking GDP, crippling cuts to entitlement programs, tax hikes and with more than half of all young citizens unemployed. A frightening picture of life on the edge of fiscal insanity and social instability:

> *Hundreds of thousands of Greeks began a 48-hour nationwide strike on Tuesday, shutting down schools, banks, local government offices and ports to protest the government's latest round of austerity measures. Transportation in Athens became difficult as subway and taxi services were halted and flights in and out of the country were stopped for three hours early in the day. State hospitals were running on emergency staff.*

While strikes and public unrest unfolded, Greece was inching closer and closer to uncontrolled bankruptcy.[20] The government was rapidly losing what was left of its sovereignty to run its own country. It put its last ounces of hope in one last austerity package, as explained by *Der Spiegel*:

---

19 "Eve of austerity: strikes consume Greece ahead of new cuts," *Der Spiegel*, November 6, 2012. Available at: http://www.spiegel.de/international/europe/strikes-cripple-greece-ahead-of-austerity-vote-in-parliament-a-865609.html, accessed December 27, 2013.
20 Please see: http://libertybullhorn.com/2012/11/05/greece-verging-on-uncontrolled-bankruptcy/, accessed December 27, 2013.

> *In addition to further tax hikes and cuts to pensions, the expected*
> *measures will raise the retirement age from 65 to 67 and make it easier*
> *to fire or transfer civil servants. Altogether they are aimed at saving the*
> *state €13.5 billion ($17.3 billion) and are a key condition of Greece's*
> *international creditors to continue to receive emergency bailout funds.*

In addition to grim statistics, austerity has been a force of brutal destruction in Europe, unleashing merciless devastation on the economies where it has been put to work. While destroying whatever people get from government, it entraps them in dependency on the destroyed services by continuing to take the same taxes from them. The Greek people have even less of their own money today to provide for themselves what government promised but is no longer delivering.

Austerity is the gateway to industrial poverty.

Alas, a story from Ekathimerini on October 1, 2012 depicted a society in tailspin.[21] A society in rapid decline is an easy victim for extreme political movements. In Greece, the neo-Nazi party known as Golden Dawn has been quick to capitalize on the devastation that austerity has left in its wake. Once again, a report from the *Guardian*, this one from September 28, 2012:

> *Greece's far-right Golden Dawn party is increasingly assuming the role*
> *of law enforcement officers on the streets of the bankrupt country, with*
> *mounting evidence that Athenians are being openly directed by police*
> *to seek help from the neo-Nazi group, analysts, activists and lawyers*
> *say. In return, a growing number of Greek crime victims have come*
> *to see the party, whose symbol bears an uncanny resemblance to the*
> *swastika, as a "protector". One victim of crime, an eloquent US-trained*
> *civil servant, told the Guardian of her family's shock at being referred*
> *to the party when her mother recently called the police following an*
> *incident involving Albanian immigrants in their downtown apartment*
> *block. "They immediately said if it's an issue with immigrants go to*
> *Golden Dawn," said the 38-year-old, who fearing for her job and safety,*
> *spoke only on condition of anonymity.*

It is difficult to say what will come out of this crisis. The best outlook is that Greece can stabilize its parliamentary democracy and limp along with its new,

---

21 Please see: http://www.ekathimerini.com/4dcgi/_w_articles_wsite1_1_01/10/2012_463996, accessed December 27, 2013.

significantly lower standard of living. The worst outlook is that the country continues its slide into economic despair and social chaos. This in turn would open up for dedicated radicals such as Golden Dawn to seize power.

If that happens—if Nazis once again get to rule a European country—then anything is possible.

At least for now, though, it looks like Greece is temporarily stabilized. In November of 2012 the EU–ECB–IMF troika reached a deal with Greece. The deal defused the imminent risk of the country tail-spinning into uncontrolled bankruptcy. British newspaper the *Guardian* reported on November 27 that the troika had released emergency cash, allowing the Greek government to pay its bills for a little while longer:

> *European governments and the IMF sought to bury months of feuding over Greek debt levels in a tentative agreement that should see the release of up to €44bn in bailout funds needed to rescue Athens from insolvency. But after almost 12 hours of talks for the third time in a fortnight between eurozone finance ministers, leaders of the IMF, the European central bank and the European commission struggled to reach a consensus, suggesting a lack of confidence that the effort to resurrect the Greek economy will bear fruit or that three years of European bailout policy was working.*

This deal did not change anything as far as the underlying crisis goes. Nothing the troika—or the Greek government—did during 2012 changed the variables that caused the crisis. The welfare state is intact, still making the same spending promises as before the crisis, though with partial defaults in the form of cuts to health care, medical drug subsidies, etc. The Greek taxpayer is shouldering an even heavier burden now than he did before.

Somewhere, the parties involved in the debt talks to save Greece seemed to be aware of this when they made their deal. The only thing they could muster was a plan to ease the burden of debt and give Greece a little bit more time to breathe. The *Guardian* again:

> *The meeting agreed to shave projected Greek debt to allow it to level at 124% of GDP by 2020, entailing a 20% cut in Greek debt by the deadline. With the IMF demanding a writedown of Greece's debt by its official eurozone creditors and Germany leading the resistance to such a move, declaring it illegal, the meeting agreed on a mixture of*

measures involving debt buybacks, lower interest rates on loans, longer
maturity periods on borrowing, and ECB returns to Greece of profits on
its holdings of Greek bonds.

At the end of the day, though, all that this accomplished was yet higher tensions
between EU member states over an increasingly insoluble crisis. The *Guardian*
again, this time its Economics Blog:[22]

> *[There] has been an acceptance that Greece needs additional help to*
> *make its debt sustainable. The IMF has been making the point that*
> *Greece is going through an immense amount of pain for no purpose,*
> *since tax increases and spending cuts to reduce the budget deficit are*
> *being outweighed by the revenue loss from a country five years into a*
> *brutal depression.*

As for the reference to the IMF, on November 1, 2012 the *Greek Reporter*
explained:[23]

> *Efforts to rescue Greece have failed to provide the basic structural*
> *reforms needed to help bring competitiveness to its economy, said*
> *John Lipsky, the International Monetary Fund's former first deputy*
> *managing director. "It has been frustrating because some of these*
> *have been clear from the outset in so many ways," Lipsky said in*
> *an interview in Copenhagen Oct. 31, according to Bloomberg.*
> *"I feel this process could have been handled so much better." Europe is*
> *pressuring Greece to step up efforts to rein in its deficit and deregulate*
> *the economy. The austerity measures are exacerbating the nation's*
> *economic pain and won't lay the foundation for a lasting recovery,*
> *Lipsky said.*

Yet as of May 2013, the Greek government is still trying to put new austerity
measures in place.

---

22 "Greek bailout deal is a classic fudge – but should work for now," *Guardian*, November 27,
    2012. Available at: http://www.guardian.co.uk/business/economics-blog/2012/nov/27/greek-
    bailout-deal-should-work-for-now, accessed December 27, 2013.
23 Please see: http://greece.greekreporter.com/2012/11/01/lipsky-efforts-to-rescue-greece-have-
    failed/, accessed December 27, 2013.

Spain

Table 4.2   Spain

	2009	2010	2011	2012	2013	2014
Private consumption growth	-0.3	1.1	2.1	1.4	1.9	1.1
Youth unemployment	37.8	41.6	46.4	53.2	–	–
Consumption share of GDP	55.9	56.4	55.7	55.7	–	–
Taxes to GDP	35.1	36.6	35.7	36.4	–	–

Source: Eurostat.

In June of 2012 the EU was beginning to panic over the disastrous government budget situation in Spain. The national government was hemorrhaging money as scores of unemployed and poor flocked to its welfare state's entitlement programs. Taxpayers, on the other hand, were fewer and farther in between; the youth unemployment figures reported in Table 4.2 above tell a chilling story to that effect.

The leaders of the EU and their troika allies, the ECB and the IMF, really had no reason to panic over Spain. In the summer of 2012 the Spanish government was hard at work carrying out the latest round of austerity dictates from the EU–ECB–IMF troika. The leaders of the troika, in turn, had by that time had years to study the consequences of their policies on Greece and had no reason at all to be surprised, let alone go into panic, over the fact that the same thing was happening in Spain.

Still, they reacted the exact same way as they had with Greece. In an attempt to avoid a complete meltdown of the economy, the EU opened the bailout floodgates with emergency loans in exchange for more austerity promises.[24] Just like Greece, Spain had to implement both tax increases and spending cuts. And just like in Greece, austerity set off a spiral of political turmoil:[25]

> Spanish police fired rubber bullets and charged protestors in central Madrid early Friday at the end of a huge demonstration against economic crisis measures. The protest was one of over 80 demonstrations called by unions across the county against civil servant pay cuts and

---

24 Please see: http://libertybullhorn.com/2012/06/11/saving-spain-europe-opens-bailout-floodgates/, accessed December 27, 2013.
25 Please see: http://ca.news.yahoo.com/spain-workers-plan-mass-demos-against-cuts-181530139. html, accessed December 27, 2013.

tax hikes which drew tens of thousands of people, including police and firefighters wearing their helmets. "Hands up, this is a robbery!" protesters bellowed as they marched through the streets of the Spanish capital. At the end of the peaceful protest dozens of protestors lingered at the Puerta del Sol, a large square in the heart of Madrid where the demonstration wound up late on Thursday.

[The protests] were the latest and biggest in an almost daily series of demonstrations that erupted last week when Prime Minister Mariano Rajoy announced measures to save 65 billion euros ($80 billion) and slash the public deficit. Among the steps is a cut to the Christmas bonus paid to civil servants, equivalent to a seven-percent reduction in annual pay. This came on top of a pay cut in 2010, which was followed by a salary freeze.

Again with a chilling parallel to Greece, the austerity measures—among them a 7 percent pay cut for public employees and an increase in the value-added tax—came on top of other, earlier measures. And just like in Greece, these new cuts had no impact on the trajectory of the Spanish government's deficit. On the contrary, the net result was more unemployment, more poverty—and more people depending on government.

More people went from being taxpayers to being entitlement consumers.

Somehow, some Spaniards saw this already last summer. AFP-Yahoo News again:

"There's nothing we can do but take to the street. We have lost between 10 and 15 percent of our pay in the past four years," said Sara Alvera, 51, a worker in the justice sector, demonstrating in Madrid. "These measures won't help end the crisis."

Some of the measures she referred to were a cut in unemployment benefits and an increase in the top value-added tax bracket from 18 to 21 percent. These are measures with direct consequences for how much, or how little, households spend. It is therefore easy to predict that private consumption in Spain will grow much below 2 percent in the next couple of years.

Another easy prediction is rising social and political tensions in the wake of austerity. Reuters, September 26, 2012:[26]

> *With protesters stepping up anti-austerity demonstrations, Rajoy presents painful economic reforms and a tough 2013 budget on Thursday, aiming to persuade euro zone partners and investors that Spain is doing its deficit-cutting homework despite a recession and 25 percent unemployment. Figures released on Tuesday suggested Spain will miss its public deficit target of 6.3 percent of gross domestic product this year, and on Wednesday the central bank said the economy continued to contract sharply in the third quarter.*

Predictably, the austerity policies proved ineffective against the economic crisis. There was no change for the better in sight, which prompted investors in Spanish Treasury bonds to question the government's credit status. The Spanish government had to respond with interest rates in the 7.4–7.5 percent bracket, dangerously close to junk status.

Higher interest rates escalated an already serious mortgage crisis, forcing people out of their homes and saddling many of them with life-long debt.[27] This crisis accelerated to such proportions that on November 15, 2012, Yahoo News could report that government had made an emergency intervention:[28]

> *Spain approved a two-year suspension of evictions Thursday for some needy homeowners unable to pay their mortgages, but activists said the government failed to address the larger issue of how those who give up their homes may still remain indebted, sometimes for the rest of their lives. Evictions have suddenly became one of the most sensitive topics in Spain's financial drama, and government officials acted less than a week after a Spanish woman facing eviction killed herself by jumping from an apartment balcony. They are trying reverse or at least delay a trend that has seen more than 371,000 mortgage eviction orders issued since the financial crisis hit the country in 2008.*

---

26 "Rajoy inches toward aid as protests seethe," Reuters, September 26, 2012. Available at: http://www.reuters.com/article/2012/09/26/us-spain-rajoy-idUSBRE88P09F20120926, accessed December 27, 2013.

27 Please see: http://www.testosteronepit.com/home/2013/4/16/the-new-nazis-of-spain.html, accessed December 27, 2013.

28 "Spain halts evictions of the needy after suicides," AP-Yahoo News, November 15, 2012. Available at: http://news.yahoo.com/spain-halts-evictions-needy-suicides-193425479--finance.html, accessed December 27, 2013.

It is important to once again point to the real cause of this crisis. It was not the result of something that evil, capitalist banks invented, but had instead an origin comparable to the American mortgage meltdown: a combination of poorly designed policy measures together with the ideologically charged idea that everyone has the right to own a home.[29]

Part of the evidence for this is further down in the Yahoo News story:

> The government, which is still preparing a broader overhaul of the country's mortgage and property laws, said it hoped to shield those most in need by suspending mortgage payments for mortgage holders with annual income of €14,400 ($18,400) or less after taxes, or those with expired unemployment benefits.

How do you get a mortgage if you make $18,400 per year? Even in Spain, that is not a whole lot of money, especially if we take into account that the national income tax rate in Spain begins at 24 percent (24.75 percent after recent tax increases).[30] Then you pay provincial taxes, local taxes, value-added taxes on everything you buy ...

Now, a friend of common sense might ask the pertinent question: who is going to pay all the mortgages that hundreds of thousands of Spaniards can no longer pay? Part of the answer is the same as here in the United States after our mortgage crisis: taxpayers.

It is hardly a surprise, therefore, that during 2012 Spain was boiling with unrest and severe political tensions, including stepped-up campaigns in some provinces to secede from Spain.

On July 25, 2012 the British newspaper the *Daily Mail* summarized the situation:[31]

- panic may spread from Spain to Italy and tear the euro-zone apart;

---

29 Please see: http://www.cablegatesearch.net/cable.php?id=05MADRID1088&q=spain, accessed December 27, 2013.
30 Please see: http://www.expatfinancialadvicespain.com/Spanish-Tax-Rate-2012.htm, accessed December 27, 2013.
31 "Spain edges closer to disaster as the euro crisis spreads (and Greece is facing a 1930s-style depression)," *Daily Mail*, July 23, 2012. Available at: http://dailym.ai/NIL7vy, accessed December 27, 2013.

- British taxpayers could be dragged into a bailout of stricken Spain;

- FTSE 100 index of leading shares down 2 percent as Spain bans short-selling of shares to stem stock market losses;

- French and German markets down 3 percent;

- Italy heads towards bailout with nearly £1 trillion public debt;

- Spanish sovereign borrowing costs soar to crisis levels: 10-year bond yields at 7.5 percent, unsustainable in medium term.

The *Daily Mail* also noted, ominously:

> *The Eurozone was back on the brink last night as Spain edged towards a financial disaster that could tear the single currency apart. Analysts said Spain's huge economy was at a "tipping point" and would inevitably need international aid. In a sign that Europe's debt crisis is deepening, Italy's borrowing costs edged higher, Greece was facing a 1930s-style depression and its austerity measures were said to be faltering.*

At that time, in the middle of the summer of 2012, Spain was in dire need of EU-backed loans of up to 100 billion euros. Its banks were suffering from a property speculation crisis, then had to deal with the fact that the 408 billion euros they had invested in Spanish Treasury bonds were not as safe and secure as they had thought.

The renewed mortgage crisis, partly a result of austerity, added a dimension to the Spanish crisis that the Greeks did not have to deal with. Another unique Spanish ingredient is provincial secessionism, which was also fueled by harsh austerity measures. Independence movements in some Spanish provinces, with the wealthy Catalonia in the lead,[32] were quick to exploit the national government's tough budget cuts.

The separatist movements in Spain are strong and they got a big boost as people turned to them in anger over the national government's austerity policies. In August of 2012, as the national government started putting its austerity package to work, some regional governments refused to cooperate:[33]

---

32 Please see (subscription required): http://on.ft.com/1fh3wg1, accessed December 27, 2013.
33 Please see: http://euobserver.com/economic/117135, accessed December 27, 2013.

An escalating dispute between Madrid and Spain's regional authorities risks undoing its austerity pledge to EU authorities. The conflict erupted on Tuesday (31 July) when Jose Antonio Grinan, the President of the Andalucia region, walked out of a meeting of Madrid's Council of Fiscal and Financial Policy when it told him to cut another €3 billion from his 2012 budget. Catalonia boycotted the meeting in the first place, saying it already cannot pay some hospital, child-care and elderly-care centre workers.

Regional politicians obviously took the opportunity to capitalize on rising sentiments of provincialism, but they also had their own reasons to resist austerity:

Asturias and the Canary Islands voted against the council's demands. The Basque region also raised heckles. Regional spending was the main reason why Spain last year missed its deficit targets under EU rules: Andalucia and Catalonia between them have a GDP of €346 billion, or 32 percent of the country's total economy. Andalucia's Grinan renewed his attack on the government on Wednesday. He said at a press conference in Seville, the Andalucian capital, that he would challenge Madrid's demands in Spain's Constitutional Court if need be.

There is also an open ideological dimension to this:

The Socialist also fired a political broadside against conservative Prime Minister Mariano Rajoy. "This … could close 19 hospitals, all of the Andalucian health service, or get rid of 60,000 public workers, one in four of the local governments workforce," he said at the press event, according to local news agency Europa Press. "We are taking resources away from health care and education to save the banks, that is intolerable."

As the national government continued to push through its austerity package, resistance among the general public grew stronger. The situation gradually got desperate, to a point where the Spanish prime minister found himself in the same situation as his Greek colleague before the May parliamentary election.[34]

In September of 2012 a march for independence for Catalonia gathered hundreds of thousands of people, with the central government's austerity

---

34 Please see: http://euobserver.com/economic/117352, accessed December 27, 2013.

policies as a rallying cause.[35] On October 22, 2012, Helena Spongenberg, expert on Spanish politics with the *EUobserver*, explained that the regional elections held a day earlier in the Basque Country and Galicia further raised regional tensions and contributed to a chaotic political landscape:[36]

> *The past year's austerity measures taken by the current Spanish government – led by President Mariano Rajoy's centre-right Partido Popular – got the thumbs up in Galicia [It] was feared that voters in Galicia would take their anger of Madrid's severe budget cuts out at the polls, as it happened at the regional election in Andalusia in March when the Social Democrats defeated PP. The fears were unfounded and PP has even increased its absolute majority gaining 41 (previously 38) seats out of 75 in the Galician Parliament ... The election in the Basque Country, however, turned out as expected – or rather, as feared by the government in Madrid. Two out of three lawmakers in the Basque Parliament are now Basque nationalists – 48 seats out of 75 ... The moderate nationalist party PNV was the overall winner with 27 seats, and is set to form a minority government in Vitoria ... PNV backs further regional autonomy from Madrid, but [PNV leader] Urkullu also promised in the election rally to bring a new law on Basque independence to a referendum in 2015.*

Spongenberg saw this as a temporary mandate for the national government to proceed with austerity. But Prime Minister Rajoy got a rude awakening when on November 25, 2012, two-thirds of the voters in Catalonia supported a referendum on independence.[37]

In other words, Spain's austerity policies has reinforced separatism and could, if continued, put the nation's unity in jeopardy.

The question that Spanish voters should ask themselves is whether or not the welfare state is so dear to them that they are willing to risk the unity of their country to save it. That is, after all, the essence of what the national government is saying when it continues to impose austerity on the Spanish economy.

---

35 Please see: http://www.euractiv.com/future-eu/catalans-march-independence-news-514743, accessed December 27, 2013.

36 Please see: http://blogs.euobserver.com/spongenberg/2012/10/22/breathing-space-and-headache-at-spanish-regional-elections/, accessed December 27, 2013.

37 Please see: http://www.huffingtonpost.com/2012/11/25/catalan-elections-2012_n_2187770.html, accessed December 27, 2013.

As noted earlier, there is no alternative in relying on the "rescue fund" as an alternative to austerity. Not only does the "rescue fund" come with all the negative consequences outlined here, but the Spanish government will in all likelihood have to double down on its austerity policies in order to get any money. That would create a double-whammy for the Spanish economy: short-term destruction of growth and jobs, and long-term threats of inflation.

It is sad to see an entire continent commit macroeconomic suicide. It is even sadder when it is happening in the name of an ideology. But the saddest part of it all is that the alternative—structural reform to end the welfare state—could so easily be done, with excellent results for everyone, especially the poor, needy and unemployed.

As things stood at the end of 2012, only one obstacle seemed to stop the separatists from gaining critical momentum. Technically, the EU could (would) require Catalonia to apply for separate membership with the EU, or choose to stay out of the Union.

That said, given the trajectory that the entire EU project is on, the Catalonians might actually view secession from Spain as well as the EU to be a blessing. Hopefully, it would mean that the people of Catalonia would not have to humiliate themselves the way many middle-class Spaniards have had to do during the recession. From the CNBC on September 25, 2012:[38]

> *On a recent evening, a hip-looking young woman was sorting through a stack of crates outside a fruit and vegetable store here in the working-class neighborhood of Vallecas as it shut down for the night ... The young woman was looking through the day's trash for her next meal. Already, she had found a dozen aging potatoes she deemed edible and loaded them onto a luggage cart parked nearby ... The woman, 33, said that she had once worked at the post office but that her unemployment benefits had run out and she was living now on 400 euros a month, about $520 ... She was squatting with some friends in a building that still had water and electricity, while collecting "a little of everything" from the garbage after stores closed and the streets were dark and quiet. Such survival tactics are becoming increasingly commonplace here, with an unemployment rate over 50 percent among young people and more and more households having adults without jobs.*

---

38 "Spain recoils, as its hungry forage trash bins for a next meal," CNBC, September 25, 2012. Available at: http://www.cnbc.com/id/49162890, accessed December 27, 2013.

According to Eurostat data, the spending on welfare programs increased in Spain from 19.5 percent of GDP in 2001 to 25 percent in 2009. If we listen to what the advocates of the welfare state often say, namely that it will always be there for the poor and needy in hard times, then with such a surge in spending in such a short period of time, the Spanish welfare state should have been well prepared for the crashing economy.

It was not. It ran into a deep deficit the instant the recession hit. The deficit was then exacerbated by the austerity dictates from the EU–ECB–IMF troika. Toward the end of 2012 the situation was so bad, in fact, that the EU launched a "rescue fund" dedicated to salvaging whatever could be salvaged from Europe's crumbling welfare states. It was born out of a good theoretical idea: set aside money to assist deficit-stricken EU member states so that "regular" government funding would not be affected. The problem is that whenever we are dealing with big government, theory and practice rarely match. The countries that the rescue fund would help are not in some temporary trouble that will pass with a little fiscal band aid. They are going to need aid for a very long time, and the "treatment" mandated by the EU–ECB–IMF troika is perpetuating the need for aid.

As a result, the "rescue fund" will become a permanent funding tool for welfare states that make more promises than they can keep. Since the fund needs money from somewhere and that is probably not going to be the troubled welfare states, the fund will in effect end up becoming a redistribution mechanism for money from "well run" welfare states to the troubled ones. Nothing will change in practice, except that taxpayers in "well run" welfare states will have to give away even more of their hard-earned money to the government.

The EU seems to want to get around this, at least temporarily, by having the ECB print money that will go directly into the rescue fund. This pumps out new money supply at a time when demand for money is very low. The short-term effect of this is a depreciation pressure on the euro: when the euro falls versus other big currencies, import prices start rising. This can cause capital flight if investors fear that the depreciation is long-term. As a result stock markets are depressed and it becomes even harder to sell euro-denominated Treasury bonds.

Another effect is that import prices accelerate, driving inflation at a time when the economy is in a bad recession. This would not be a problem worth noticing if it was not for the fact that there is a significant risk that the EU will have to make the rescue fund permanent. Because of that, any funding through the monetary printing press will eventually unleash monetarily driven inflation—and a lasting one at that.

To further bump up this inflation threat, the European Central Bank made a critical, and potentially catastrophic, decision during the fall of 2012: in order to save Greek and Spanish Treasury bonds from the junk yard the ECB made a promise to always buy whatever amount of bonds that bond-holders wanted to sell.

A promise to buy an unlimited amount of Treasury bonds is akin to a promise to print an unlimited amount of money. Theoretically, the only cap is the amount the Spanish government owes its creditors. In practice, there is no firm limit, because the ECB has promised to buy any amount of Treasury bonds which in effect allows Spain to accumulate as much debt as it desires.[39]

In fact, with austerity driving up debt rather than capping it as intended, Spain could theoretically be looking at a future similar to that of Argentina or Venezuela. The difference of course is that both of those nations have their own currencies, but Argentina has been de facto dollarized for a long time, and the euro is not as ironclad a protection against inflation as many European leaders seem to believe. Spain needs to fund its runaway budget deficit one way or the other, and even if the country is too small to provoke a wave of monetary inflation through its monetized deficit, it could easily sink to Venezuelan levels if it left the currency union.

There is nothing on the horizon today to precipitate secession, but so long as the crisis continues in Europe the institutional confidence in the euro will gradually erode. Eventually, the question of who stays in the currency union and who goes will become an urgent one.

As a matter of fact, the rescue fund itself might accelerate the demise of the euro. The fund essentially promises to feed government spending with expanding money supply. (It is extremely unlikely that the fund can sustain for any period of time if funded by tax revenues.) The practical meaning of this is that welfare states like Greece, Spain, Portugal and Italy can continue to dole out work-free income—aka entitlements—to large groups of citizens.

---

39 Absurdly, as is explained in Chapter 5, on the macroeconomic consequences of the crisis, this might be the best that could happen to the Spanish economy.

These entitlements are then used to pay for daily expenses, which of course keeps consumer demand at a reasonable level. But the flip side is that the more people are allowed to remain on entitlements, the fewer people will participate in the workforce. As fewer participate in the workforce, there will be less production to go around, which means less supply compared to demand—an inflation driver right there—and fewer taxpayers.

As the taxpaying population shrinks, whether in absolute or relative terms, the government's need for rescue-fund bailout cash increases. The European Central Bank, created as a bastion of inflation busting, will then find itself trapped in endless money supply expansion. Its only collateral will be Treasury bonds in such abundance that you would have to pay people to take them off your hands.

If the ECB continues to stand by its perpetual-purchase program for troubled government bonds, there will come a point where investors begin fleeing the euro in droves.

But the looming debacle of the rescue fund is not the only financial problem hanging over the Spanish capital. It also has its mortgage crisis to deal with, created in good part by the same social-engineering policies that brought about America's mortgage meltdown. In November of 2012 the Spanish government intervened and forced a suspension of mortgage payments for qualified homeowners. This accumulated a pile of bad loans which, after EU intervention, were concentrated to one single bank. The idea was that this bank should sell off its assets at highly discounted prices and thus create a controlled deflation of the bad-assets balloon.

The problem with this strategy is that it would require private investors to buy shares in the bank, something they were not willing to do. On November 16, 2012, *El Confidencial* reported:[40]

> *that the so-called "bad bank" will manage nationalized real estate and mortgages, but not for the purpose of promoting socially motivated housing. To recover losses, hope is set to time, with the bank having 15 years to eliminate the need for its own existence.*

---

40 Please see (in Spanish): http://www.elconfidencial.com/economia/2012/11/16/economia-amplia-un-mes-el-plazo-para-que-entren-inversores-en-el-banco-malo-109392/, accessed December 27, 2013.

It remains to be seen if that strategy will work. The blog Zerohedge commented:[41]

> In other words, not only was the Spanish government caught lying (hardly notable these days), but just as we expected, over two weeks after the launch of "Sareb"—the latest deus ex which was supposed to offload the need to issue ever more sovereign debt to fund Spain's nationalization of ever more insolvent sectors to private investors, said private investors have taken a long, hard look at the "deal" the Bad Bank offers them and have said "no bid." Oh yes, and so much for "vehicle credibility."

The Spanish government, backed by the Eurocrats in Brussels, had to start looking for another taker of the bad debt. It is almost a tautology to say that this "other taker" will be the EU through one of its bailout initiatives—either for banks or for governments.

While the government was struggling to get its mortgage crisis under control, that very same crisis had repercussions for the budget deficit as well. The *Wall Street Journal*, October 1, 2012:[42]

> The Spanish government said the effort to clean up an ailing banking system will widen its budget gap and increase its debt load. The admission comes as concerns mount over the country's solvency, sending its borrowing costs soaring and pushing the government of Prime Minister Mariano Rajoy closer to requesting European Union aid to help it finance itself. The euro zone's fourth-largest economy is grappling with the collapse of a decadelong housing boom that sent tax revenue plummeting, cratered domestic demand and saddled banks with billion of euros of bad debts.

With the exception that the deficit has its origin in the welfare state and was exacerbated by the mortgage crisis, the *Wall Street Journal* makes a good point. The newspaper then explains:

---

41 Please see: http://www.zerohedge.com/news/2012-11-16/minor-glitch-emerges-spanish-bad-bank-deployment-no-investor-interest, accessed December 27, 2013.

42 "Spain expects a wider budget gap," *Wall Street Journal*, October 1, 2012. Please see (subscription required): http://online.wsj.com/article/SB10000872396390444138104578028484168511130.html, accessed December 27, 2013.

In its 2013 budget plan presented to Parliament on Saturday, the government said that the bank aid will inflate its budget deficit to around 7.4% of gross domestic product [for 2012], which is above the deficit target of 6.3% of GDP for 2012 it has committed to with the European Union. Spain said that if the effect of measures to help banks are excluded, it would meet its EU commitment.

Even as a forecast for 2013, this is highly unlikely. Austerity continues, even after the regional backlash. As the *Wall Street Journal* noted:

The budget revisions come as Mr. Rajoy faces mounting social and political backlash against his austerity and economic-reform measures. On Saturday, thousands of demonstrators descended on the national Parliament in Madrid for the third time in the past week to protest against spending cuts and tax increases ... Spain's austerity budget for 2013 includes tax increases and spending cuts worth €13 billion by the central government. Including previously announced measures and cuts to be implemented by regional and municipal governments, Spain aims to slash its budget deficit by €37 billion next year. Even so, many analysts believe a deep economic recession will make it difficult for Spain to meet its EU commitments to reduce the deficit to 4.5% of GDP in 2013 and to 2.8% in 2014.

And who will be left to bail out the ailing welfare states when they hit that second (or in some cases third) recession dip? German taxpayers, of course. That, in turn, will only raise tensions further in Europe: in November of 2012 the Germans were beginning to feel the pinch of Europe's massive austerity wave,[43] with a second recession dip looming on the German horizon.

---

43 Please see: http://libertybullhorn.com/2012/11/16/austerity-hits-germany/, accessed December 27, 2013.

Italy

Table 4.3   Italy

	2009	2010	2011	2012	2013	2014
Italy	0.5	1.5	2.0	1.9	1.4	1.2
Youth unemployment	25.4	27.8	29.1	35.3	–	–
Consumption share of GDP	60.4	60.3	60.2	59.0	–	–
Taxes to GDP	46.5	46.1	46.2	47.7	–	–

Source: Eurostat.

On July 13, 2012, Euractiv reported that Moody's credit rating institute had downgraded "Italy's government bond rating by two notches to Baa2 and warned it could cut it further, piling on pressure just hours before the country launches its latest bond sale. The move left Italy's rating just two notches above junk status and could raise already painful borrowing costs."[44] This put Italy in the same category as Greece and Spain, with a cumulative effect of all the downgrades that had a negative effect on the euro, which is already under stress. Euractiv continued:

> The stark warning from Moody's, which highlighted Italy's vulnerability to political shocks in the eurozone and could deepen worries about the region's debt crisis, knocked the euro down about a quarter of a cent to $1.2190 in Asian trade. "Italy's government debt rating could be downgraded further in the event there is additional material deterioration in the country's economic prospects or difficulties in implementing reform," the agency warned in a statement. "Should Italy's access to public debt markets become more constrained and the country were to require external assistance, then Italy's sovereign rating could transition to substantially lower rating levels."

According to Eurostat, Italy has one of the worst debt-to-GDP ratios in the industrialized world (see Figure 4.2).

---

44 Please see: http://www.euractiv.com/euro-finance/moodys-cuts-italy-credit-rating-news-513882?utm_source=EurActiv%20Newsletter&utm_campaign=c919ff8ab7-newsletter_weekly_update&utm_medium=email, accessed December 27, 2013.

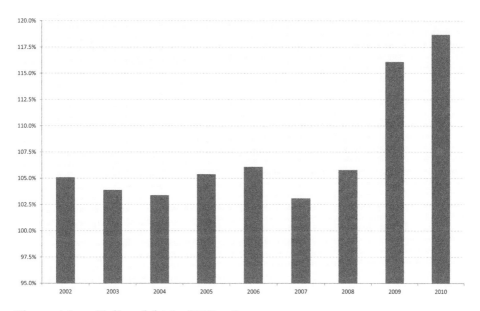

Figure 4.2   Italian debt-to-GDP ratio
Source: Eurostat, www.ec.europa.eu/eurostat.

In other words, the downgrade should come as no surprise.

Repeating a spell-casting pattern from other welfare states, the Italian government was saved from a very awkward moment of embarrassment by the country's own banks, who according to Malaysia-based *Business Times* absorbed a good part of the new debt:[45]

> *Italian banks came to the rescue yesterday [July 13] after the country suffered a ratings downgrade, but while Rome cut its three-year borrowing costs at auction, a rise in 10-year bond yields highlighted concern it may fall victim to Europe's debt crisis. Moody's cut Italy's sovereign debt rating to Baa2 yesterday, citing doubts over Italy's long-term resolve to push through much-needed reforms and saying persistent worries about Spain and Greece were increasing its liquidity risks. Solid domestic demand helped the Italian Treasury sell the top planned amount of 5.25 billion (RM20.37 billion) in bonds, paying less than a month ago on three-year paper.*

---

45 Please see: http://www.btimes.com.my/Current_News/BTIMES/articles/itest/Article/, accessed December 27, 2013.

Before this bond sale banks had already entrusted the Italian government with a lot of money. Again according to Eurostat, from 2008 to 2010 financial institutions increased their share of total Italian government debt from 38.6 percent to 44.5 percent. That is an increase of more than 180 billion euro in two short years—and a huge problem when the Treasury bonds turn into high-risk assets.

The bond sale, of course, was only one leg in a long, panic-stricken march for Italy through 2012. On August 8 the *EUobserver* reported:[46]

> *Italian Prime Minister Mario Monti won a confidence vote on Tuesday (7 August) linked to another €4.5 billion worth of spending cuts aimed at convincing investors that Italy's economy is sound. But fresh data shows a worsening recession and rising borrowing costs. The bill – which comes on top of previous spending cuts amounting to a total of €26 billion by 2014 – was approved with 371 MPs, while 86 said No and 22 abstained. The €4.5 billion worth of cutbacks will be implemented by the end of this year. The remaining €21.5 billion are to be spread out over the next years. Thousands of hospital beds are to be slashed and 20 percent of top public officials to be fired as part of the austerity drive.*

At that time, Italy was experiencing a 0.7 percent quarter-to-quarter contraction in its GDP. Having to pay 6 percent on its Treasury bonds, the Italian government was teetering dangerously close to the junk yard.

After the EU–ECB–IMF troika opened its rescue-fund faucet, Italy's interest rates fell to somewhat more modest levels around 4.5 percent. Then, in December 2012 the *Daily Telegraph* reported:[47]

> *The FTSE Mib in Milan fell by as much as 3.5pc to 15,157.72 on Monday after the technocrat prime minister said he would resign as soon as crucial budget legislation was approved. Italian borrowing costs also rose. The yield on 10-year government bonds climbed by almost 0.3 percentage points to 4.8147pc, while the cost of insuring Italian debt against default rose by 27 basis points to 285bps. This means that it now costs £285,000 a year to insure £10m of debt over five years ... The*

---

46 Please see: http://euobserver.com/economic/117183, accessed December 27, 2013.

47 "Debt crisis: markets dive after Mario Monti announces resignation," *Daily Telegraph*, December 10, 2012. Available at: http://www.telegraph.co.uk/finance/financialcrisis/9734204/ Debt-crisis-markets-dive-after-Mario-Monti-announces-resignation.html, accessed December 27, 2013.

*resignation also sparked a wider sell-off. Madrid's IBEX 35 index fell
2.3pc, hit also by rising bond yields in debt-laden Spain.*

There is one feature to the Italian crisis that makes it different from the crisis in Spain: the Italian prime minister in 2012, Mario Monti, was appointed by the EU. This is like the president of the United States appointing the governor of New Jersey, a power grab that is as disturbing to many Europeans[48] as it would be a cause for revolution in the United States. Nevertheless, the power grab continues and expands, so far with the sole purpose of fixing a member state's finances.

However, it is easy to draw the conclusion that the EU leadership has power ambitions far beyond fiscal technicalities. When they deposed the Italian government and put their own man in charge, they displayed an unhealthy desire to grab even more power from the EU member states. This is a very high-risk game, though. For a while during the winter of 2013 it looked like Italy would exit the euro-zone. Eventually, it stayed in, but only after yet more power play by the EU leadership. Evidently, they put more value on keeping the currency union intact than on the well-being of the citizens of individual member states.

Italy left 2012 in bad shape, with the prospect of an election that would not create any governable parliamentary majority (that proved to be true). Add to that the following numbers, and the situation for Italy going through 2013 is verging on disastrous (on each point the Italian economy has to return to its 2005 levels before we can safely say that it is out of its recession):[49]

- *social benefits as share of GDP*: 25.4 percent in 2005; 28.4 percent in 2009 (latest year available);

- *youth unemployment*: 24 percent in 2005; 29.1 percent in 2011;

- *real GDP growth*: average 2004–08 was 1.06 percent per year; average 2009–13 including forecast is -0.86 percent per year;

- *government as share of GDP*: 47.9 percent in 2005; 51.4 percent in 2010.

---

48 Please see: http://euobserver.com/political/118438, accessed December 27, 2013.
49 Eurostat: http://epp.eurostat.ec.europa.eu/portal/page/portal/eurostat/home, accessed December 27, 2013.

The last number is particularly important. When viewed in the context of the meager—to say the least—GDP growth rates, the growth in the relative size of government tells us two things.

First, there have been no real efforts at reforming away government spending programs in Italy. On the contrary, the austerity policies that have been in place over the past few years have served the purpose of preserving the welfare state and its big spending programs. As a result, the burden that government places on the private sector will not get lighter in the next few years. That alone basically rules out an economic recovery.

Second, the GDP share of government in Italy was down to 49.9 percent in 2011, a 0.5 percent reduction over 2010. In 2010 the Italian economy grew by 1.8 percent, but growth fell back to 0.4 percent in 2011 with a preliminary -1.4 percent in 2012. These numbers clearly indicate that the reduction in government GDP share in 2011 was not caused by a sustained trend in GDP growth, but instead the result of austerity-driven spending cuts executed in 2010. In 2011 and 2012 those cuts took effect and turned the economy downward again after the "growth spurt" in 2010.

A further indication that the Italian government is not retreating from the economy is that general government revenue as share of GDP is slowly trending upward. It was 43.4 percent in 2005 and 46.1 percent in 2011. When government revenue as share of GDP is growing, and government spending as share of GDP is falling, then government is taking more from the economy while giving less back.

This organized net drainage of resources from the private sector into government is also known as austerity.

The bottom line, then, is that:

1.   the Italian finance minister has set a policy goal that means "full employment first, then a stop to austerity";

2.   every conceivable indicator shows that Italy is neither near nor on a trajectory toward full employment; and that

3.   austerity will continue to stifle any economic recovery in the Italian economy.

Since austerity serves the purpose of preserving the welfare state, one has to ask: is this ideological behemoth so important to Europe's politicians that they are willing to drive their economies into the deepest of depression ditches just to be able to say "I saved the welfare state"?

Chapter 4b

Europe in 2012:
Deeper into the Crisis

As explained in Chapter 4a, the crisis did significant damage to the three main southern member states of the European Union. This chapter shows that those countries were not the only ones to suffer.

France

Before we delve into France's share of the turbulent events of 2012, let us first examine some numbers related to our quantitative assessment of industrial poverty. Due to lack of consistency in data quality across all countries discussed in this chapter, the numbers span only a few years. However, the period is enough to give us a first glance of what the recession has done to these countries in terms of economic stagnation (see Table 4.4).

Table 4.4   France

	2009	2010	2011	2012	2013	2014
Real consumption growth	-0.1	1.2	1.9	1.6	1.4	1.8
Youth unemployment	23.9	23.6	22.9	24.3	—	—
Consumption share of GDP	57.0	56.9	56.1	56.1	—	—
Taxes share of GDP	49.2	49.5	50.6	51.7	—	—

Source: Eurostat.

While, again, these numbers are from a deep recession, the real question is whether or not France—and the other countries discussed here—will perpetuate their tepid economic performance. Using Sweden, again, as our reference point we can stipulate that if austerity is used to eliminate the budget deficits that these countries are struggling with, it is very likely that an emerging state of industrial poverty could very well turn into their perennial future.

As the *EUobserver* reported in July of 2012, France has indeed followed in the Swedish footsteps:[1]

> *The French government will have to find €43bn in order to bring the country's deficit in line with EU rules by 2013, a fresh report has shown. A report on state finances by the national Court of Auditors said Paris will need to find up to €10bn this year and €33bn next year to reduce its budget deficit to 4.5 percent of GDP and then 3 percent of GDP. "The situation remains extremely worrying," court president Didier Migaud told Le Monde newspaper, referring to the state of the country's public finances. When asked how the money for 2013 will be found Migaud said "with more rigour."*

In short, "austerity" of the same kind that the Greek government has put to work. To date (the spring of 2013) France has yet not been hit as hard as Greece, but the reason for this is not that the French economy is more resilient. Simply put, France has not been in the austerity business for quite as long as Greece has.

Based in part on the Greek experience, the EU report from the summer of 2012 sparked an intense debate in France over how the country should deal with its budget deficit. As the *EUobserver* article explains, the socialist president, Francois Hollande, who was elected in May of 2012, had his own idea of what to do:

> *The large sums are set to test Socialist President Francois Hollande's skills of persuasion. He was elected in May on an anti-austerity ticket – although he always maintained that he would stick to France's deficit-cutting promises. But the report also shows that the battle will be even harder than expected – and some form of austerity will be needed. The auditors suggested next year's economic growth will be 1 percent, well short of the 1.7 percent predicted by the previous government while public debt is set to reach 90 percent of GDP by the end of the year – a level economists say affects growth. Under EU rules, countries have to keep their debt below 60 percent.*

---

1   Please see: http://euobserver.com/economic/116836, accessed December 27, 2013.

Later in July there was more to come:[2]

> *French lawmakers Thursday [July 19, 2012] backed a series of measures abolishing tax breaks and taxing the wealthy as the new Socialist government pursued efforts to kickstart the economy with a tax-and-spend programme. The measures were part of the first budget bill presented by President Francois Hollande's government since he unseated right-wing Nicolas Sarkozy in May with pledges to focus on growth instead of austerity.*

But there was not much focus on growth in their tax policies. The National Assembly ended Sarkozy's moderately growth-oriented "work more, earn more" tax law which exempted overtime hours from income and payroll taxes. The French lawmakers also voted for the now-notorious extra tax on wealth above 1.3 million euros. Other growth-hampering measures included in the tax package were a 37 percent reduction in the exemption ceiling for inheritance tax (down to 100,000 euros), the introduction of a new 3 percent tax on cash dividends and an increase in the financial transactions tax from 0.1 to 0.2 percent.

It should not come as a surprise that high-earning French entrepreneurs and professionals flooded London real estate agents during 2012, and allegedly still do.[3]

President Hollande's belief that his country needs economic growth is well founded. From 2010 through the Eurostat forecasts for 2013 and 2014, the French economy will average 1 percent GDP growth per year. And that is before revisions adjusting for job losses in the wake of higher taxes.

The problem is, there is no economic research that shows that higher taxes stimulate GDP growth. Not even Hollande and his socialists believe this— their hope is to get more growth from more government spending. But the *absolutely best* that government can do is produce something less efficiently, less tailored for people's needs than what the free market would do. With more money going to government the tax base will eventually shrink, whereupon the purpose of the tax increase is forfeited.

---

2   Please see: http://ca.news.yahoo.com/french-lawmakers-abolish-tax-breaks-boost-taxes-rich-204249429.html, accessed December 27, 2013.

3   Please see: http://libertybullhorn.com/2012/05/05/wealth-flight-from-france-if-socialist-wins/, accessed December 27, 2013.

Even if government spent every dime it takes in from higher taxes, the end result would be a loss in both ends: less work and investment due to higher taxes and less production due to the fact that government is a monopolist with coercively earned revenues, not an agent on a free market.

That said, it is a sad fact that statists like the French socialists are not inclined to listen to facts. They are still going to maintain their defense for higher taxes. Their last line of defense is entirely ideological: they are more interested in saving their welfare state than getting the economy up in gear.

Since the French welfare state was running out of money already before President Hollande was elected, it is rather easy to see what the true motive was behind their rush to raise taxes. The only difference between the ideologically driven tax hikes in France and the austerity disaster in Greece is that the French are living the illusion that government spending can get them to a better end result. Officially, their argument was that more government spending would stimulate the private sector and bring the economy back to growth and full employment. But if you raise taxes by $100 and grow government spending by $100, all you have done is shuffle $100 around in the economy. Furthermore, since you spent every dime of what you took in from your higher taxes, you end up with the same budget deficit as before.

The only way for the French to get anywhere with their higher-taxes-and-higher-spending model was to raise taxes even more than they increased spending. In other words, to raise taxes by, say, $120 but only increase spending by $100, using the extra $20 to reduce the budget deficit. One of their tax-hike ideas was the 75 percent "hate tax" on incomes above one million euros.

But now the problem is that government takes even more out of the private sector than it gives back. As a result, private-sector activity is depressed beyond what any (inefficient) government spending program could possibly compensate for. The French have experienced this, especially when they have tried to put their hate tax to work: people with incomes that would be targeted by the tax started fleeing to Belgium and England. The tax base eroded and government did not get nearly as much as it was hoping to from the tax.

None of this was really news at the time when the French socialists won the election in 2012. What seemed to have escaped them was the simple economic truth that that so long as you raise taxes it does not matter all that much if you increase or decrease government spending.

This, however, began dawning on them in early 2013. In April, the *Daily Telegraph* reported:[4]

> *French president Francois Hollande is facing an anti-austerity revolt from his own ministers as he pushes through a fresh round of tax rises and austerity to meet EU deficit targets. Three cabinet members have launched a joint push for a drastic policy change, warning that [spending] cuts have become self-defeating and are driving the country into a recessionary spiral. "Its high time we opened a debate on these policies, which are leading the EU towards a debacle. If budget measures are killing growth, it is dangerous and absurd," said industry minister Arnaud Montebourg. "What is the point of fiscal consolidation if the economy goes to the dogs. Budget discipline is one thing, cutting to death is another," he said.*

This does not mean that France's socialists have seen the light and are beginning to turn their back on big government—the root cause of this crisis. All it means is that they want to have a more lenient budget policy so they can continue to grow government.

But their reason for fearing what austerity will do to their country is important: they see nothing but social and economic decline in Southern Europe, with the Italian and Spanish crises right on their borders. They fear the consequences of similar social unrest and political turmoil in their own country. They are getting increasingly desperate about putting their country back on track again, but the measures they propose—the statist ideas that characterized President Hollande's run for office in early 2012—will do no such thing for them.

On the contrary: more government is the last thing Paris should try. If it stays on its present course, France is destined for industrial poverty.

---

4   Please see: http://www.telegraph.co.uk/finance/financialcrisis/9999148/Francois-Hollande-faces-austerity-revolt-from-own-ministers.html, accessed December 27, 2013.

Cyprus

Table 4.5   Cyprus

	2009	2010	2011	2012	2013	2014
Private consumption growth	1.2	2.0	3.4	2.7	1.6	1.7
Youth unemployment	13.8	16.7	22.4	27.8	–	–
Consumption share of GDP	66.0	66.1	66.2	65.8	–	–
Taxes to GDP	40.1	40.9	39.7	40	–	–

Source: Eurostat.

Of all member states of the EU, Cyprus has been doing among the best. The data reported in Table 4.5, which again is from the first years of the recession, shows that the Cypriot economy has been dealing with the crisis relatively well. Based on the numbers reported here, economic theory would have it that with private consumption constituting a relatively large share of GDP there is solid, stable domestic demand and thereby a private jobs market.

A moderate tax-to-GDP share reinforces this impression. Together, the two numbers would suggest that Cyprus has an opportunity for a private-sector driven recovery that economies with higher taxes and smaller private-consumption sectors do not have.

Unless, of course, austerity gets in the way.

Which it did. Cyprus was hit hard when the 2012 austerity crisis swept like a bonfire across the southern rim of Europe. On July 3, 2012, CBS News reported:[5]

> *Cyprus says it has begun talks with officials from the European Union and the International Monetary Fund to gauge how much money it needs from the EU bailout fund for its troubled banks. The Finance Ministry said in a statement Tuesday the officials will meet with government and central bank authorities, as well banking officials, union leaders and politicians over the next few days. It said the meetings are only exploratory and that no negotiations on possible austerity measures*

---

5   Please see: http://www.cbsnews.com/8301-505245_162-57465536/cyprus-starts-bailout-talks-with-eu-imf-officials/, accessed December 27, 2013.

will be held yet. Cyprus last week became the fifth EU country to ask
for financial aid from its partners in the common currency union.

This was, of course, the lead-up to the Cyprus Bank Heist, when the Cypriot government (strong-armed by the EU and the European Central Bank) seized 40 percent of bank deposits above 100,000 euros. But unlike what the mainstream media has said, the bank crisis was not primarily the result of some global financial crisis.

It was caused by the Greek government.

Cyprus has very close ties to Greece. What is commonly referred to as "Cyprus" is really the western part of the island. The Mediterranean island Cyprus is split in two parts, separated by a UN buffer zone. The western part is a sovereign nation, commonly referred to as Cyprus, with Greek as its official language. The eastern part is a Turkish province and one of the poorest territories in Europe.

The close economic ties between Cyprus and Greece motivated Cypriot banks to invest heavily in Greek Treasury bonds.[6] During 2012, the Greek bond became a toxic asset, which created a huge problem for Cypriot banks. Treasury bonds in general are used by banks to create a reliable low-risk base for their portfolios; when Treasury bonds become high-risk assets they can no longer rely on their portfolio management strategies.

In other words, what goes around comes around. In 2011 the EU forced those who owned Greek Treasury bonds to accept a "write-down," that is, to forgive up to 50 percent of the debt that Greece owed them.[7] As a result, the Cypriot government found itself facing a systemic bank failure. It needed to bail out the banks, turning again to taxpayers for more cash. That deprived the private sector of even more money, causing yet more decline in private-sector activity, which erodes the tax base, which increases the government's need to borrow ...

---

6   "Insight: why did Cypriot banks keep buying Greek bonds?" Reuters, April 30, 2013. Available at: http://reut.rs/11SeNNH, accessed December 27, 2013.
7   "EU's Greek gamble: 50-percent bank debt write-off," *Russia Today*, October 27, 2011. Available at: http://rt.com/news/greek-debt-write-off-843/, accessed December 27, 2013.

Portugal

Table 4.6   Portugal

	2009	2010	2011	2012	2013	2014
Private consumption growth	-1.0	1.0	1.9	0.0	1.0	0.7
Youth unemployment	24.8	27.7	30.1	37.7	—	—
Consumption share of GDP	64.2	64.6	63.1	61.5	—	—
Taxes to GDP	39.6	41.6	45	41	—	—

Source: Eurostat.

On September 17, 2012, ABC News reported:[8]

> *Income taxes will go up next year, Vitor Gaspar said. Public employees will lose either their Christmas or vacation bonus, each roughly equivalent to a month's income, and many pensioners will lose both. More public employees will join the dole queue. Last year was tough enough, especially for public employees, whose salaries were cut by up to 10 percent as they lost their two bonuses. Meanwhile, property and sales taxes went up, and tax deductions and welfare entitlements went down for everyone. To top it off, the recession, which the government predicted would bottom out this year, will continue into next.*

This should not surprise anyone. An economy that is subjected to austerity will take a turn for the worse.[9] But the Portuguese government does not have to read research papers to realize this—by the time it went to work with its latest austerity package (September 2012) Greece had been in an austerity-induced macroeconomic coma for four years.

If Portugal's lawmakers and cabinet members had listened, they might have avoided the social unrest that Reuters reported on September 15, 2012:[10]

---

8   Please see: http://abcnews.go.com/International#.UFfi-0bcCII, accessed December 27, 2013.
9   Larson, S.R., *Austerity: Causes, Consequences and Remedies*, Working Paper, April 30, 2012. Available at: http://papers.ssrn.com/sol3/papers.cfm?abstract_id=2048739, accessed December 27, 2013.
10   "Portuguese and Spanish march as anger over tax hikes grows," Reuters, September 15, 2012. Available at: http://www.reuters.com/article/2012/09/15/us-portugal-protests-idUSBRE88E0GZ20120915, accessed December 27, 2013.

Over 150,000 Portuguese marched on Saturday against planned tax hikes that have shattered the consensus behind austerity imposed by an EU/IMF bailout, and tens of thousands more marched in Spain, seen as the next country needing to be bailed out ... Organized via the Internet, the rallies brought together Portuguese from all walks of life, chanting: "Out of here! IMF is hunger and misery!" and calling on the centre-right government to resign.

As yet another Greek parallel, Portuguese voters have a penchant for radical political parties. In the 2011 election three far-left parties with varying versions of socialism on their agenda gathered 41 percent of all votes. All of them share a disdain for capitalism and economic freedom, and one of them is an outright Leninist communist party.[11]

So long as the free-market economy is being blamed for the current crisis—as opposed to the welfare state which is the real culprit with its excessive spending programs—parties such as these will continue to grow all across Europe. This just a bit more than two decades after the fall of the Berlin Wall.

The problem is that radical Leninists (and neo-Nazis in Greece) represent the only visible alternative to voters who are fed up with austerity, the economic crisis and a stagnant standard of living. This is very much true in Portugal. So long as Portuguese voters are only presented with one alternative to austerity, namely more austerity, Portugal is doomed economically in the same way as Greece is.

Either that, or open Leninism.

Some Portuguese politicians seem to realize the parallels between Portugal and Greece.[12] That insight was part of what brought about the court battle over the austerity package, the content of which the BBC presented in chilling detail:[13]

The standard income tax rate is rising from 24.5% to 28.5%. The savings are Portugal's toughest in living memory, aimed at meeting

---

11 Please see: http://en.wikipedia.org/wiki/Portuguese_Communist_Party, accessed December 27, 2013.

12 Please see: http://euobserver.com/tickers/117558, accessed December 27, 2013.

13 "Portugal set for major tax rises as 2013 budget hits," BBC New Europe, December 31, 2012. Available at: http://www.bbc.co.uk/news/world-europe-20875752, accessed December 27, 2013.

*the terms of a 78bn-euro (£64bn) bailout ... Earlier Portugal's Finance
Minister, Vítor Gaspar, admitted the tax rises were "enormous", but
were "another determined step toward recovery."*

On January 2, 2013, Euractiv reported:[14]

*Portuguese President Aníbal Cavaco Silva said in his New Year
speech that he will send his country's controversial 2013 budget to
the Constitutional Court. The move could put at risk a €78 billion
bailout deal from the eurozone and IMF. "On my initiative, the
Constitutional Court will be called on to decide on the conformity
of the 2013 state budget with the constitution of the republic," the
President said.*

The Portuguese economy is in about as bad shape as the Greek economy. Its
inflation-adjusted average growth rate over the past 10 years is zero. This
latest contested austerity package is not going to improve that growth record.

The Netherlands

Table 4.7   The Netherlands

	2009	2010	2011	2012	2013	2014
Private consumption growth	0.6	1.2	1.6	1.8	2.3	1.8
Youth unemployment	7.7%	8.7%	7.6%	9.5%	–	–
Consumption share of GDP	45.7	45.1	44.2	43.9	–	–
Taxes to GDP	51.4%	51.2%	49.8%	50.4%	–	–

Source: Eurostat.

In 2012 Europe's voters voiced more resistance to austerity than any year
before. At the same time, the Eurocrats of the EU doubled down on their
determination to force deficit-running member states through the grinds
of austerity. While most of the drama unfolded in Southern Europe, other
countries also saw eruptions of anti-austerity sentiments.

---

14 Please   see: http://www.euractiv.com/euro-finance/portuguese-president-sends-count-
news-516838, accessed December 27, 2013.

On April 23, 2012 the *Daily Telegraph* reported that the Dutch prime minister had resigned after having failed to convince the parliament to accept a new austerity package:[15]

> *Mark Rutte, the Prime Minister, resigned after his fragile liberal-conservative coalition government, which has a no parliamentary majority, fell apart at the weekend after the far-right Freedom Party walked out of talks to implement £12 billion (15bn euros) in cuts. "The government now knows that it is no longer sufficiently assured of the necessary parliamentary support to do what is necessary for our national economy," he admitted in his resignation letter to Queen Beatrix. Diederik Samsom, the leader of the pro-European opposition Labour Party accused Mr Rutte of "dropping the ball at the worst possible moment" and demanded snap elections. "We have to deliver clarity to the country as soon as possible," he said.*

On May 4, 2012 the *Irish Times* elaborated:[16]

> *The multibillion-euro package of austerity cuts that brought down the Dutch minority government ... has been described by the country's economic planning agency as "too vague to assess". In an embarrassment for the caretaker coalition ahead of a September 12th general election, both the central planning bureau and economists at the ministry of finance have admitted they cannot say with certainty that the deal can meet the EU budget deficit requirement of 3 per cent of GDP ... The bureau is uneasy about the lack of supporting data on a proposed cut of €1.6 billion in spending on healthcare, which is already shaping up to become one of the more contentious issues at the polls. It also says it needs details of a "general" but unspecified across-the-board cut of €875 million. Clearly anticipating the argument that the €13 billion in cuts could hinder economic growth, it says it has not seen any government analysis of how proposed tax increases – including a rise in VAT from 19 to 21 per cent, aimed at generating €3.2 billion – will affect consumer spending or jobs.*

---

15 "Dutch prime minister Mark Rutte resigns over austerity measures," *Daily Telegraph*, April 23, 2012. Available at: http://bit.ly/Ih46b3, accessed December 27, 2013.

16 Please see (subscription required): http://www.irishtimes.com/news/dutch-austerity-package-too-vague-1.514069, accessed December 27, 2013.

In August the *EUobserver* reported that the Dutch socialists were slightly ahead in the polls.[17] This was logical given the popular and parliamentary resistance to austerity: socialists all over Europe, including the Netherlands, have been opposed to austerity because it involves cuts in government spending. However, the Dutch socialist alternative to EU-imposed austerity, as presented by the *EUobserver*, was not exactly a better alternative for the Dutch people:

> *Last week, the Socialist party leader Emile Roemer promised to hold a referendum on the fiscal compact treaty, describing it as "idiotic" to impose a 3% limit on budget deficits. The treaty, which was designed by Merkel and former French President Nikolas Sarkozy, and enthusiastically backed by Rutte, would put the deficit and debt brakes from the Stability and Growth Pact into national constitutions.*

The 3 percent rule has been part of the EU constitution since the Maastricht Treaty was signed more than 20 years ago, so if a Dutch government under socialist majority would walk away from that rule, it would deliberately be in breach of the EU constitution. But that technical detail aside, any austerity defiance on behalf of the Dutch would in all likelihood be met with the same iron fist from the EU as the Greeks, Spaniards, Italians, Cypriots and Portuguese have experienced.

By the time the Dutch election came around on September 12, 2012, an eerie silence had thrown a wet blanket over Europe. The continent was catching its breath, though in the immediate vicinity of some real trouble:

- in the Greek election voters narrowly re-affirmed their support for status quo but gave authoritarian parties 40 percent of the votes;

- French voters redesigned the country's political landscape by handing both the presidency and the national parliament to the socialists;

- Spain received new austerity marching orders from the EU and put them to work, jeopardizing the very unity of the country; and

- there was rapidly growing resistance in Germany toward helping other EU member states, as the country's own economy began showing worrisome signs of slowing down.

---

17 Please see: http://euobserver.com/political/117329, accessed December 27, 2013.

The Dutch crisis, with frustrated voters and anti-austerity politicians on one side and EU-loyal, "responsible parent" politicians on the other, served as a good illustration of a growing divide in Europe. The EU loyalists were essentially being reduced to errand runners for the Eurocracy, having to bear the brunt of the burden of forcing austerity upon their fellow citizens.

On the other side of the divide were the voters, taxpayers and consumers of government services, feeling increasingly shortchanged by a government they see taking more of their money while giving less back. In France the socialists successfully rode on this wave of voter resentment, and as mentioned they looked like winners in the Netherlands a few weeks out of the election. All they had to do was preach against the previous prime minister's austerity policies.

Other EU-skeptical parties gained ground using the same strategy. This put the pro-austerity, EU-friendly parties in a difficult position. In this latter group were the social democrats and center-right liberals, both dominant in Dutch politics. Basically, they only had one chance if they wanted to win the election, and that was to adopt austerity-skeptical rhetoric.[18]

They also distanced themselves from the EU policy of bailing out countries in deep crisis, a strategy that eventually proved to work. They won, but not by much.[19]

This outcome reinvigorated the politicians and Eurocrats who were pushing for more austerity, but also for a more centralized—and politically more unaccountable—Europe. For every country that the EU leadership could put under its thumb by dictating austerity policies, they expanded their domains of power and control.

It became increasingly clear during 2012 that this was precisely the direction that the Eurocracy wanted to take Europe. Right after the Dutch voters had marginally chosen to re-elect a pro-EU government the de facto (unelected) president of the EU, a Mr. Herman van Rompuy, actually went public with the ambition to further centralize government powers in Europe:[20]

---

18 Please see: http://www.euractiv.com/elections/dutch-pm-greece-get-financial-he-news-514632, accessed December 27, 2013.
19 "Dutch election: pro-Europe VVD and Labour parties win," BBC News Europe, September 13, 2012. Available at: http://www.bbc.co.uk/news/world-europe-19566165, accessed December 27, 2013.
20 Please see: http://euobserver.com/institutional/117527, accessed December 27, 2013.

> *EU Council chief Van Rompuy on Wednesday (12 September) tabled
> an "issues paper" on how to further integrate the eurozone, including
> a common budget, limited debt mutualisation and a parliamentary
> assembly ... This is supposed to "get member states out of the closet
> on the most sensitive issues," one EU official told this website. Drafted
> with the heads of the EU commission, European Central Bank and
> Eurogroup of finance ministers, the paper proposes "a central budget
> for the euro area" in order to "deal with asymmetric shocks and help
> prevent contagion."*

Europe already has the largest governments in the world. Mr. van Rompuy
and his fellow Eurocrats want to create yet another layer on top of fiscally
obese member-state governments. Once he gets what he wants and the EU
becomes a formal government with the right to tax and spend, it will do
exactly that: tax and spend.

This is bad enough, and reason enough for Europe's EU skeptics to resist
further expansion of EU powers. But not only is the growth of an EU-level
government a problem—the nature of government spending makes that growth
even more problematic. Just like in the United States, most of the money that
Europe's governments spend goes toward entitlements. This means that as
the EU centralizes control over spending, it will also centralize control over
entitlements.

Entitlements mean a welfare state. What is really happening is therefore
that Europe is slowly moving in the direction of a massive, continent-wide,
European-sized welfare state, controlled by bureaucrats in Brussels and
dispensing entitlements to 500 million people. In other words:

- a centralized unemployment system with centralized reimbursement rates;

- a centralized health care system where Brussels is the single payer as well as the dictator of how many doctors there can be, where they can practice and what they can practice, including what medical procedures Europeans can and cannot get at their hospitals;

- common euro-denominated Treasury bonds issued on the good credit of Germany to fund bad credit for Greece (aptly characterized by Cato senior fellow Dan Mitchell as co-signing a loan for your unemployed, alcoholic cousin[21]); and, of course,

- a centralized tax system where the EU imposes its own taxes either on top of those already levied by national governments.

A pan-European welfare state, run through the fiscal equivalent of central heating from the bureaucratic offices in Brussels, will not solve a single problem that led to Europe's current economic crisis. On the contrary, all it will do is elevate the crisis to the EU level and thereby remove the differences between member states that have thus far kept most of the EU member states on the right side of a total meltdown.

We are not talking some half-measured American welfare state here. No, this is as big a government as you will see this side of the Berlin Wall: government runs schools all the way up through the university level; it runs and pays for all health care, all elderly care and almost all child care. Government also provides all citizens with general income security, far up and beyond anything we have seen here in the United States.

And this is just for those who have a job. For Europe's tens of millions of unemployed, life means total and utter subjugation to government bureaucracies: unemployment offices, job training offices, job placement programs on a job market where every job attracts hundreds of applicants.

When the next crisis hits—if Europe survives this one—the panic-driven, austerity-laden response is going to hit the lives of half-a-billion people. But even before that happens, this almost Soviet-style centralization of powers will have far-reaching, negative effects on the European economy. A welfare state run by Brussels will force taxpayers in wealthier EU member states to cough up the money for entitlements going to citizens in less-wealthy member states. The "bailouts" for countries like Greece that the EU put in place during 2012 are a crude ad-hoc version of what this welfare state would look like. In the bailout program taxpayers in primarily Germany are paying for endless unemployment and welfare programs in Greece, Spain and Portugal. Under a centralized welfare state, the redistribution from "north" to "south" would be made permanent.

---

21 Please see: http://danieljmitchell.wordpress.com/2012/05/23/eurobonds-the-fiscal-version-of-co-signing-a-loan-for-your-unemployed-alcoholic-cousin-who-has-a-gambling-addiction/, accessed December 27, 2013.

It is clear from the aforementioned *EUobserver* story that this is not some pie-in-the-sky idea, but a realistic scenario for the future.[22] An EU Summit in the fall of 2012 gave the go-ahead to parts of the van Rompuy paper that did not require a change to the EU constitution. There is no doubt that Europe's political leaders share the opinion that you should never waste a good crisis ...

The Czech Republic

Table 4.8   The Czech Republic

	2009	2010	2011	2012	2013	2014
Private consumption growth	-4.4	4.5	3.4	-0.8	1.3	1.3
Youth unemployment	16.6%	18.3%	18.0%	19.5%	—	—
Consumption share of GDP	48.9	48.2	47.6	46.9	—	—
Taxes to GDP	44.7%	43.7%	43.0%	44.5%	—	—

Source: Eurostat.

On November 6, 2012, the *Prague Monitor* reported that austerity-motivated budget cuts proposed by the Czech parliament had run into resistance from all corners of the economy:[23]

> *The Czech government Monday interrupted its debate on the draft 2013 state budget until Wednesday ... Businesses, academics and most ministries have voiced disagreement with the draft. Reservations were also voiced by the LIDEM party, a minor coalition government member. Its representatives are against the cuts in the sphere of transport ... "We have proposed the cuts in the individual [budget] chapters purely technically. It is a technical proposal the government is discussing," Finance Minister Miroslav Kalousek (TOP 09) said, adding that it was essential not to exceed the budget deficit of 3 percent of GDP.*

This is the cap from the European Union's Stability and Growth Pact. It is forcing every member state to shift focus as it goes into a recession, away from trying to stop the recession and on to trying to cap and reduce the budget deficit. Austerity is designed for this purpose, not to promote economic growth, a fact

---

22 Please see: http://euobserver.com/institutional/117527, accessed December 27, 2013.
23 Please   see: http://praguemonitor.com/2012/11/06/government-interrupts-budget-debate, accessed December 27, 2013.

that according to the *Prague Monitor* the legislators in the Czech Republic are becoming painfully aware of:

> *The cuts would affect science and research, transport infrastructure, teachers' salaries and programmes co-financed from the EU funds, among others. The government must submit the draft budget to the Chamber of Deputies by November 23. The revised version of the budget bill has taken into account the latest economic outlook and the failure to push through a tax package raising both VAT rates by 1 percentage point. The tax package has been tied to a vote of confidence in the coalition government of Necas (Civic Democrats, ODS). The Chamber of Deputies is to vote on the package on Wednesday.*

These are the same policies that have been so unsuccessfully tried in Greece, Spain, Portugal, Ireland, Netherlands, Italy and even Hungary. Austerity was the last thing the Czech economy needed: through the recession years 2009–12 its GDP growth rates averaged 0.5 percent, with outlooks of about 1 percent per year for 2013 and 2014.[24]

Unfortunately, the link between austerity and tepid or negative growth seems to be absent in the Czech public debate. Another story from the *Prague Monitor* adds comments from analysts who express concerns about the austerity measures—but only when it comes to the loss of government spending:[25]

> *The cutting of the expenditures of the Czech state budget for next year by Kc41bn [$2bn] will lead to a worsening of the economic development in the Czech Republic, analysts have told CTK in a poll. The new state budget draft, whose discussion the cabinet Monday put off until Wednesday, reckons with a drop in revenues and expenditures for next year by Kc41bn. It keeps the state budget deficit at Kc100bn [$5bn]. David Marek, an analyst at company Patria Finance, believes that cuts in investment will from a shorter-term point of view cause significantly greater harm in the economy than the hike in value added tax (VAT) that was originally proposed.*

This makes no sense at all. If the government is spending money on investments, then it is calculating on a long-term return for the economy, not a short-term

---

24 Eurostat, National Accounts Statistics, available at: http://epp.eurostat.ec.europa.eu/portal/page/portal/national_accounts/introduction, accessed December 27, 2013.
25 Please see: http://praguemonitor.com/2012/11/06/analysts-budget-cuts-worsen-economic-development, accessed December 27, 2013.

benefit. An increase in the value-added tax, on the other hand, inflicts harm on the economy virtually overnight.

Perhaps Mr. Marek needs to re-examine his analysis of the two policy measures. That said, it is important to remember what the real problem is here. The choice is not between spending cuts and tax hikes, but between austerity and an orderly retreat of government on all fronts. That orderly retreat means structural spending cuts combined with appropriate tax cuts, executed over a period of several years. The goal is to allow the private sector to grow, step in and replace what government has previously monopolized.

Back to the *Prague Monitor*:

> *Representatives of entrepreneurs Monday rejected the cuts in state budget expenditures stimulating growth. They disagree with the restrictions on spending on support of research, export, co-financing of structural funds and transport infrastructure construction, Confederation of Industry president Jaroslav Hanak told CTK. Transport Ministry spokesman Martin Novak said the cuts in the budget of the State Transport Infrastructure Fund (SFDI), that have been proposed by the Finance Ministry in the new budget draft, will jeopardise the construction of the D3 motorway from Prague to the Austrian border and the further modernisation of the most dilapidated sections of the D1 motorway from Prague to the Polish border via Brno.*

It is common that politicians who want to preserve their welfare state go after spending that has nothing to do with entitlements and income redistribution. Even from a libertarian viewpoint it is possible to make the case that government should provide infrastructure. Therefore, highways and possibly even railroads may fall within the realm of essential government functions. Income redistribution, on the other hand, does not. The Czech government runs social welfare programs equivalent to 20 percent of the nation's GDP, which tells us that there is quite a bit of room for reforms oriented at reducing the size of government.

Hopefully the Czech economy is not going to follow in the same footsteps as other welfare states in Europe. But with habitual austerity as the governing fiscal policy regime, and with an economy on the edge of negative growth, the outlook is not exactly positive.

Chapter 5

Can Austerity Work?

So far we have seen plenty of reasons to dismiss austerity as a general policy rule. It has made the current European crisis escalate from bad to worse, and it had a clearly negative impact on the Swedish economy in the 1990s.

With such discouraging evidence, should we forget austerity completely? Contrary to what the previous chapters may indicate, the answer is: no, we should not dismiss austerity entirely. Instead of discarding it from the deck of fiscal policy strategies, we should take a close look at alternative approaches to austerity. But more than that, we need to build a broader theoretical understanding of the scope and limitations of austerity policies, regardless of their composition. To do so we need to elevate our inquiry to the level of general economic theory.

As for the composition of austerity measures, many studies suggest that when austerity is biased in favor of spending cuts rather than tax increases, it is much more likely to succeed. If those studies are correct, then the Swedish experience would have been very different; the package that the social-democrat government implemented came with two dollars of tax hikes for every dollar of spending cuts. The exact opposite balance could, in other words, have brought about a more positive macroeconomic outcome.

By the same token, the recommendation for Europe would be to concentrate on spending cuts.

The following section analyzes four key studies concluding that spending-biased austerity is preferable and has a good chance of success.

A problem with pro-austerity studies is that they are not entirely consistent in defining the success of austerity measures. To reinforce the results from these studies, another section of this chapter brings in economic theory to help, asking: can we use Austrian and Keynesian economic theory to better understand whether or not austerity can be successful?

The last section goes back to the Swedish case. The purpose is to analyze, with a life-size example, whether or not there is any merit to the suggestion that spending-cuts-only austerity is more successful than tax-biased austerity.

The Anti-Keynesian Hypothesis

Austerity studies that conclude in favor of spending cuts typically do so based on a hypothesis that lower government spending today causes a rise in private-sector spending tomorrow. This hypothesis is directly contradictory to prevailing macroeconomic theory, according to which there is a negative multiplier effect from government spending cuts to private consumption (and private business investments). It is therefore appropriate to label this the anti-Keynesian hypothesis.

Not all studies on austerity and spending cuts use this hypothesis to define success. Sometimes the definition of success is merely a reduction of the budget deficit, a success variable that is so narrow and so close to the exact content of spending-biased austerity that the result is basically trivial. A slightly expanded version of this success measurement, a drop in the debt-to-GDP ratio, makes no tangible difference.

If our research on austerity is going to meaningfully inform policy decisions, we need a more complex and dynamic definition of success. The anti-Keynesian hypothesis fits this definition.

An early study using the anti-Keynesian hypothesis was published by Giavazzi and Pagano in 1990 for the National Bureau of Economic Research (NBER).[1] They looked for evidence of austerity success in data from, primarily, Ireland and Denmark during the 1980s. Their findings are inconclusive:

> *The Danish experience shows that cuts in government spending can be associated with increases in consumption even after controlling for wealth and income, and even in the presence of a substantial increase in current taxes. The Irish case, however, highlights the potential importance of liquidity constraints for the operation of this mechanism. When current disposable income effectively constrains consumption,*

---

1   Giavazzi, F. and Pagano, M., *Can Severe Fiscal Contractions be Expansionary? Tales of Two Small European Countries*, NBER Working Paper #3372, May 1990. Available at: nber.org, accessed December 27, 2013.

> *Keynesian textbook propositions seem to recover their predictive power,*
> *as witnessed by the 7% drop in real consumption in 1982 during the*
> *first Irish stabilization.*

This gets pretty technical, and rather quickly. In order for the anti-Keynesian hypothesis to be true, the rise in private consumption following austerity would have to be driven by disposable income. This is important, especially with the Swedish experience in mind. There, when austerity set in households rapidly depleted their savings and rapidly went into debt. If an increase in private consumption is financed with an increase in household debt, it shows that consumers are not better off as a result of austerity. More likely, it is a sign that consumers have postponed enough spending needs and basically cannot wait anymore. (Your dripping ceiling cannot continue to leak water forever.)

If on the other hand the increase in private spending is driven by a rise in disposable income, then we do have a traditional Keynesian effect. If this happens when the cause is austerity focused on spending cuts, then we have found evidence of the anti-Keynesian hypothesis.

Again, Giavazzi and Pagano are inconclusive here. Their Irish example with its disposable-income constraint refutes the hypothesis. But what about Denmark? The authors report that the austerity programs from Denmark in the early 1980s "can be associated with increases in consumption." However, once again household credit enters the picture. Before we get there, though, Giavazzi and Pagano have something to say about monetary policy:

> *[Part] of the expansionary effects of the fiscal contractions analyzed*
> *here must be attributed to the concomitant monetary disinflation, that*
> *in these countries operated via the switch to fixed exchange rates with*
> *a low-inflation currency ... and the liberalization of capital flows.*
> *This produced a sharp fall in interest rates: in the presence of inflation*
> *inertia, the latter translated into a corresponding drop of real rates and*
> *a rise in aggregate demand.*

This is a factor independent of austerity, though Giavazzi and Pagano do not make this entirely clear. Strictly speaking, the legislatures and central banks in both Ireland and Denmark could have changed their monetary policies in the direction of disinflation and then deregulated capital flows without having to combined it with austerity-driven fiscal policy measures. That would in all likelihood have had an expansionary effect on consumer spending and business investments.

A word of caution, though: such a strategy would to a limited extent have had the same expansionary effects on the Danish and Irish economies as the "Quantitative Easing" monetary policy of the Federal Reserve has had on the American economy over the past few years. Monetary expansion rarely, if ever, has any substantial, lasting positive effects on economic activity; the instrument is simply too vague.

However, a deregulation of consumer credit can transmit an expansionary monetary policy—even of the indirect kind known as deregulation of capital flows—into a temporary rise in private consumption. If the deregulation is combined with austerity, then statistically it can look as though austerity had a positive effect on private consumption.

It is precisely this "correlative mistake" that Giavazzi and Pagano are concerned about. In their favor, though, it deserves to be noted that a monetary policy that fixes the exchange rate and ties it to a low-inflation target can reinforce consumer and entrepreneurial confidence. This in itself could have a positive effect on consumer spending and could conspire with capital-flow deregulation to give the private sector a healthy boost in activity.

Again, Sweden offers an example that to some degree reinforces this aspect of the Giavazzi–Pagano paper. The Swedish austerity experience was preceded by a large exchange-rate depreciation which, in turn, had substantially positive effects on economic activity. The following growth in exports had limited effects on the rest of the economy. There are many reasons for this, one of them being that the big currency depreciation was *not* followed by a fixed exchange rate. In short, during the austerity years 1995–98 Swedish monetary policy did not offer the same stable low-inflation environment as it did in the examples from other countries cited by Giavazzi and Pagano.

When an economy shifts from high inflation to low inflation, consumers gradually adjust their expectations and—once they find the low-inflation environment credible—increase their spending out of any given disposable income.[2] If it becomes easier to access consumer credit, the positive effect is reinforced.

---

2   For an empirical study providing some evidence toward this, see: Larson, S.R., *Uncertainty, Macroeconomic Stability and the Welfare State*, Ashgate, London, 2002. Larson tests the hypothesis that fluctuating prices drive up uncertainty in consumer spending, and that a high degree of uncertainty causes consumers to minimize spending in order to maximize their cash at hand. A high-inflation environment is one example of such an uncertain environment.

Again, it is possible to argue that this can all happen without the involvement of austerity. A counter-argument would be that a monetary policy that focuses on low inflation, fixed exchange rate and capital-flow deregulation creates an economic environment resilient enough to handle austerity. This is an entirely plausible interpretation of the results reported by Giavazzi and Pagano, especially since it is almost impossible to avoid a negative impact on household disposable income in a modern welfare state. One of the structural problems with our welfare state is, after all, that it gets itself deeply involved in practically every corner of the economy and of our daily activities. Thus, any kind of austerity, regardless of whether it is spending-biased or focused on tax hikes, will have a negative effect on disposable income:

- cuts to entitlements reduce disposable income by shrinking the sum total of post-tax cash in consumers' pockets;

- cuts to government employment moves well-paid employees to unemployment—even if this is temporary, it means less spending by those who lose their jobs;

- reduced or terminated government spending on investments such as infrastructure and real estate means fewer jobs for government contractors, whose workers either have to take a pay cut or go on unemployment.

These examples do not present a case against government spending cuts. On the contrary, it is critical that Europe's and North America's welfare states shrink. However, these examples remind us how careful a spending-cut surgeon's knife has to work through the economy in order to minimize collateral macroeconomic damage.

Part of that damage is to drive consumers into debt as they try to compensate for lost disposable income. Giavazzi and Pagano recognize that access to credit plays a decisive role in how consumers respond to austerity. In Denmark during the 1980s austerity period, private consumption seemed for a while impervious to contractionary fiscal policy. This could be interpreted as evidence that austerity concentrated on government spending cuts does not at all depress domestic economic activity. However, as Gravazzi and Pagano report in Table 5 (p. 20a) of their paper, Danish households borrowed massively during the 1980s. Using their homes as collateral, from 1978 to 1988 they doubled their mortgages as percent of consumer spending. For every 100 krona they spent in

1978 their mortgage loan was 94 krona; 10 years later their mortgage debt was 184 krona for every 100 krona they spent.

The conclusion, then, from the Danish example in Giavazzi and Pagano, is that we still do not have credible support for an anti-Keynesian hypothesis. The rapid rise in consumer debt in Denmark is mimicked in Sweden a decade later, suggesting that austerity in fact forced consumers into debt in order to avoid a drastic reduction in their standard of living. In Sweden, if consumers had maintained the same debt-to-disposable-income ratio they had in 1995 (the first austerity year) in the year 2000, their debt would have been 19 percent lower than it actually was.

Is it possible that the absence of austerity would have allowed Swedish consumers to spend as much as they did, or more, at this lower debt level? We will return to this question later in this chapter. For now, let us conclude that Giavazzi and Pagano do not offer any credible support for the anti-Keynesian hypothesis. To their credit, though, they do make a point of the lack of solid conclusions in their paper. It is notable that their inconclusive ending and their emphasis on the role of policies unrelated to austerity—first and foremost monetary policy—are downplayed in literature that cites their work.

In 1995 Giavazzi and Pagano made a second attempt at validating the anti-Keynesian hypothesis.[3] They analyzed data from 19 OECD countries, again publishing their results as a NBER study. They paid special attention to the Swedish economy during the period from 1990 to 1993, that is, prior to the Big Austerity Purge. They report more refined results, distinguishing between the effects of:

- on the one hand, short-term austerity and "normal" austerity measures; and

- on the other hand, very large austerity measures and protracted periods of austerity.

They conclude:

> Cuts in government consumption and in the primary deficit of "normal" dimensions tend to be associated with a contraction of private

---

3   Giavazzi, F. and Pagano, M., *Fiscal Expansions and Fiscal Adjustments in OECD Countries*, NBER Working Paper #5214, August 1995. Available at: nber.org, accessed December 27, 2013.

demand, but when the change in government consumption or in the deficit becomes very large and/or persistent, its correlation with private demand switches sign: a severe contraction tends to be associated with an increase in private demand, while abnormal budget expansions are associated correlated with private demand contractions.

From a strictly methodological viewpoint this is a good strategy. If you want to prove that event X correlates with event Y your conclusions are stronger if you can also find "mirror evidence," that is, prove that non-X will correlate with non-Y. In this case, the testing of the anti-Keynesian hypothesis would yield particularly strong results if:

1.   a very large contraction in government spending correlates with an expansion in private consumption; and

2.   a very large expansion in government spending correlates with a contraction in private consumption.

Giavazzi and Pagano (1995) do a commendable job of both analyzing their data and drawing conclusions. However, there is one big downside to building conclusions on heavy use of correlative statistics: you risk ending up with evidence that is about as useful as claiming that the green traffic light is caused by the red light because it always follows after the red light. Giavazzi and Pagano (1995) run into this problem as they try to find their "mirror evidence" according to (2) above. To prove that fiscal expansion correlates with, and conclude that it causes, a private consumption contraction, they study Sweden in the period 1990–93. This was a period when private consumption fell dramatically and the government budget went into a very large deficit.

Defining the deficit as a fiscal expansion, Giavazzi and Pagano (1995) explain:

In the Swedish case most of the action comes from a debt-financed decline in net taxes: as a fraction of potential output, public consumption is virtually stable throughout the period. This makes the Swedish experience ideally suited to test the view that a large cut in net taxes can depress private consumption and investment, rather than stimulate them as suggested by traditional textbook theory.

It is true that the Swedish tax reform in 1990 was followed by a drop in taxation. It is also true that private consumption dropped dramatically in the early 1990s.

This looks like a textbook example of a strong correlation between tax cuts and a decline in economic activity. In short: evidence for the anti-Keynesian hypothesis.

Opponents of tax cuts tend to use such evidence to argue against lowering the tax burden on consumers. Giavazzi and Pagano (1995) use it as mirror evidence for an inverse causal relationship between fiscal policy changes and private consumption. In the case of Sweden in 1990–93, both applications of this correlation are false. The reason is that the decline in private consumption had nothing to do with the decline in net taxation. There were three other reasons for it:

1.   As part of the tax reform the national government expanded its value-added tax (VAT) from having applied to about half of all private consumption to applying to all of it. The reform wanted the VAT to apply to apartment leases, newspapers and magazines, train tickets, haircuts and every other conceivable item that consumers could spend their money on. While the final shape of the VAT expansion was not quite as rigid as first planned, the application of a 25 percent tax on large, previously VAT-free spending items had a decidedly negative effect on private consumption.

2.   In good part because of the tax reform the Swedish economy experienced an inflation spike, with the inflation rate exceeding 10 percent per year for two years. Since worker compensation did not follow suit, the two-year price spike had a depressing effect on consumer spending.

3.   Unemployment went up dramatically. Its mirror image, the employment rate, is reported in Figure 2.2 above. When unemployment increases by almost one percentage point per month for a year and a half, as happened in Sweden in 1990–92, it is going to have dramatic negative effects on private spending. Those who lose their jobs will be forced to cut down on spending as their disposable income declines; those who still have jobs will adjust their expectations, hoard cash and pay off loans. We saw this expression of shifting expectations in Sweden as the household savings rate rose rapidly in the first years of the 1990s.

It is frankly a bit puzzling that Giavazzi and Pagano (1995) do not control for these variables, especially the unemployment rate, or at least give them a credible mention. They spend several pages reporting results on other control variables, such as wealth and the real interest rate. Unfortunately, most of their analysis is an exercise in regression overkill, focusing a lot of attention on a short period of time without exhaustive attention to unique events or institutional changes.

The same criticism can be applied to the other part of their paper where they study data from 19 OECD countries. One finding that seems to have some strength to it says that if austerity is protracted enough it will be followed by a rise in private consumption. More specifically, Giavazzi and Pagano (1995) imply that if government pursues austerity over an extended period of time, and then stops, private consumption will eventually increase.

Again, analytical stringency seems to have given way to correlative overkill. As mentioned earlier, the unfortunate truth is that a welfare state is deeply entangled with the private sector. Spending cuts inevitably have negative effects on consumers and entrepreneurs. Protracted spending cuts lasting for several years extend those negative effects over a long period of time. With everything the science of economics has established about consumer behavior, it is reasonable to conclude that consumers who have been under a barrage of austerity-driven government spending cuts for a sustained period of time will want to restore their long-term standard of living. (The same would hold true if they were subjected to protracted tax increases.) Therefore, it is perfectly logical that consumers increase their spending as soon as a long period of government spending cuts comes to an end.

To say that this return to a long-term consumption pattern is the result of a protracted period of austerity is to jump to conclusions. While there may be some joy and celebration involved immediately after government ends austerity, the main driving force is hardly a positive reaction to austerity per se. The net result in terms of standard of living is at best going to be zero. Giavazzi and Pagano (1995) have not taken any steps to exclude this scenario, which means that their test of protracted periods of austerity really does not prove anything other than that once austerity ends, consumers start spending.

If I subject my dog to protracted beatings, and then stop, my dog will feel better the first day I do not beat him. We could conclude that his improved mood on that day is caused by the fact that I stopped beating him. But that does not mean that me beating him has made him feel better overall.

So far, Giavazzi and Pagano, either from 1990 or from 1995, have not produced credible evidence for spending-biased austerity. This is important enough but there is one angle to Giavazzi and Pagano (1995) that could shed some light on whether or not austerity is a useful fiscal-policy strategy. We could read their results as reporting the discovery of a nothing-left-to-lose point: once government has subjected the private sector to austerity for a long enough time, consumers have been pushed to a point where they have no choice but to start spending again. Ostensibly this type of consumer reaction to austerity would be driven by a quick and significant rise in household debt.

A closer look at the data they use could produce useful tools for identifying when an economy is at, or close to, its nothing-left-to-lose point. The knowledge of such a point could be helpful in the design of future spending-biased austerity packages, as legislators would know just how much austerity an economy can take. Lawmakers in today's Greece and Spain would be well guided by such findings.

Furthermore, if we can identify a nothing-left-to-lose point it would be a contribution of evidence in favor of the anti-Keynesian hypothesis. Since Giavazzi and Pagano (1995) essentially admit that short periods of austerity do not have anti-Keynesian effects, the discovery of a nothing-left-to-lose point would reveal a "switch" in the economy, where it ceases to "act Keynesian" and starts acting "Austrian." While there is not enough evidence for the existence of a switch in the results reported by Giavazzi and Pagano (1995) there is enough material in there to inspire further research.

With the potential existence of a switch, we have come a little bit closer to proving the anti-Keynesian hypothesis. Before we continue, though, it is important to reiterate that this hypothesis is limited to fiscal policy. Even if there is evidence for the hypothesis, the central bank can pursue Keynesian monetary policy and thus either reinforce or supersede any positive economic-activity effects from austerity. It is notable that their first paper credits monetary policy and expansion of consumer credit with increasing consumer spending. Credit expansion is in fact a monetary stimulus of the economy and its positive effects on consumer spending could be taken as a validation of Keynesian theory, as opposed to the anti-Keynesian hypothesis.

Modern horizontalist monetary theory, exemplified by Basil Moore's *Horizontalists and Verticalists*, incorporates money supply into the economy to a much deeper extent than traditional monetary theory.[4] Technically, horizontalist monetary theory suggests that the money supply curve is flat and that money supply—understood as high-powered money plus liquid assets plus, at least to some degree, credit—accommodates to real-sector economic activity. Viewed this way, the credit expansion in Denmark in the 1980s and in Sweden in the 1990s and the associated continuation (first) and expansion (later) of consumer spending is a result of current economic policy, but on the monetary side, not on the fiscal side where austerity takes effect.

If, again, there is evidence of a paradigmatic switch in consumer response to austerity, could the desired positive effects show up earlier if austerity is combined with a Keynesian-style monetary policy? The answer is most likely affirmative.

Time now for the third paper seeking evidence for the anti-Keynesian hypothesis. A 2006 OECD Economics Department Working Paper by Cournede and Gonand titled *Restoring Fiscal Sustainability in the Euro Area: Raise Taxes or Curb Spending?* has been quoted as decisively verifying the hypothesis. In an article in April 2012 on the Neighborhood Effects blog at the Mercatus Institute, Matthew Mitchell claims that Cournede and Gonand present evidence "that spending-cut-focused reforms work better and are more likely to aid the economy" than any other package of austerity measures.[5]

This sounds promising indeed, even though Cournede and Gonand did not set out to primarily pursue evidence for the anti-Keynesian hypothesis. Its purpose is more narrowly to analyze the case for pension reform in Europe in view of the continent's ageing population and the need to protect governments' pension promises to future retirees. They conclude:

> *Model results indicate that if the large adjustments needed to restore fiscal sustainability were made by raising taxes, the induced distortions could entail large costs for economic growth, with most of the negative feedback coming through capital markets. The mechanism is that, if taxes are increased to finance an unchanged pension replacement rate, households have much less incentive to save and invest than if the replacement rate is reduced and taxes kept in check.*

---

4   Moore, B., *Horizontalists and Verticalists*, Cambridge University Press, Cambridge, 1988.
5   Mitchell, M., "Does U.K. double dip prove that austerity doesn't work?" Neighborhood Effects Blog, Mercatus Center, April 26, 2012. Available at: http://neighborhoodeffects.mercatus. org/2012/04/26/does-uk-double-dip-prove-that-austerity-doesnt-work/print/, accessed December 27, 2013.

There is one positive economic response to spending cuts that Mitchell presumably attributes to Cournede and Gonand, namely the increase in household savings. However, Mitchell mistakes an increase in private savings for a net increase in economic activity, a mistake that could originate in the application of Austrian theory. In reality, Cournede and Gonand apparently conclude that households will increase their savings *only to replace government-provided pensions*.

This is important for anyone leaning on their article for evidence in favor of the anti-Keynesian hypothesis. Let us look at their analysis step-by-step:

1.   In 1901 Jack makes $1,000. He pays $100 in taxes toward his future, government-provided retirement benefits. Out of his $900 disposable income he saves $100 for general purposes, leaving $800 for spending. He expects that when he retires, he can rely on the government's promise of a pension equal to 50 percent of his annual $1,000 earnings.

2.   In 1902 government decides to cut the replacement rate to 40 percent. In line with an austerity strategy biased in favor of spending cuts, government does not raise taxes. Instead it still charges the same retirement taxes as before, meaning that Jack will now get a smaller return on his $100-a-year retirement tax.

3.   How does Jack respond to this? Cournede and Gonand suggest that the cut in the replacement rate is actually going to increase savings. Therefore, we conclude that Jack will cut $20 from his annual consumption and put that money into a dedicated retirement account. This increases his personal savings by 20 percent while reducing his consumption by 4 percent.

4.   In 1903 the economy experiences a decline in private consumption. This is an inevitable effect of the increase in private savings, which in turn is a response to the government's spending cut. Does this decline in private consumption define how the economy responds to the spending cut?

5.   An Austrian economics analysis would conclude that the increase in private savings would increase private business investments, thus boosting aggregate economic activity. On the other hand, a Keynesian analysis would conclude that the decline in private

consumption constitutes a net reduction in business revenues with no promise of an increase tomorrow. Therefore, the net effect would be negative on aggregate economic activity.

Which of the two conclusions is correct, the Austrian or the Keynesian? For once the cliché-style economist answer "it depends" actually applies. The "correct" conclusion depends on what Cournede and Gonand set out to prove. That, in turn, depends on what they defined as the success of austerity. Both Cournede and Gonand as well as Mitchell in interpreting their work are primarily focused on the debt-to-GDP ratio. They show no interest in the effects of austerity on private consumption.

Even if we extend the conclusions of Cournede and Gonand to imply that a reduction in the debt-to-GDP ratio will benefit private-sector activity, there is no clear evidence in their result that this is so. The example with Jack's response to a cut in the income replacement ratio explains why no such evidence exists. Therefore, it looks like Cournede and Gonand have made it relatively easy for themselves in limiting their definition of success to something that is very close to trivial. The practical policy usefulness of their results is unfortunately limited accordingly.

This does not mean that their study is of no consequence. It begs for a follow-up concentrated on possible positive effects on private consumption from a reduction in the debt-to-GDP ratio. Keynesian theory suggests that no such effects exist, which means that any observations of a growth in private spending after the kind of austerity Cournede and Gonand study, would be clear evidence in favor of the anti-Keynesian hypothesis.

A recent paper on austerity by Alesina and de Rugy shares the same weakness as Cournede and Gonand. Alesina and de Rugy define success of austerity policy as depressing the debt-to-GDP ratio. Under the title "Austerity: the relative effects of tax increases versus spending cuts," their Mercatus Center report concludes:

> *A consensus seems to have emerged recently that spending-based fiscal adjustments are not only more likely to reduce the debt-to-GDP ratio than tax-based ones but also less likely to trigger a recession. In fact, if accompanied by the right type of policies (especially changes to public employee's pay and public pension reforms), spending-based adjustments can actually be associated with economic growth ... Fortunately, successful fiscal adjustments are possible (when mostly*

based on spending cuts and accompanied by policies that increase
competiveness) as we have seen the in the case of Germany, Finland,
and other more recent examples, such as Estonia and Sweden.

The paper is essentially a review of research by others, but there is an original contribution, again on Sweden. The paper suggests that when austerity policies have at least a two-to-one balance of spending cuts versus tax increases, the chances for success are the greatest. However, it is important again to keep in mind that their definition of success is narrowly defined as a reduction in the debt-to-GDP ratio.

Their analysis of Sweden under finance minister Anders Borg is instrumental in their pursuit of evidence that austerity can bring down the debt-to-GDP ratio. They suggest that under Borg, the Swedish government has both cut welfare spending and implemented a 20 percent cut in top marginal income tax rates. This, say Alesina and de Rugy, is evidence that austerity policies focused on spending cuts work: the cuts in welfare spending allowed for a cut in the top marginal income tax rates.

The only problem with this is that no such income tax cut has taken place. Therefore, any conclusions by Alesina and de Rugy based on their reasoning about Sweden must be deemed to be false.

However, the rest of their paper renders some credibility to the argument that spending-biased austerity has less of a negative impact on the economy. This inspires an application of a spending-biased austerity package to historic cases of austerity with a heavier bias toward tax hikes. In order to do so, though, we would have to redefine success above and beyond what could be interpreted as trivial.

Sweden in 1995–98 is an obvious candidate for testing the Alesina–de Rugy suggestion that austerity with a ratio of $2 spending cuts for $1 of tax hikes is most likely to succeed. With "success" redefined as a rise in private-sector economic activity, the next section suggests that there is some credibility to the proposal that spending-biased austerity works better than tax-biased austerity.

Another test object that could greatly help determine the strength of the Alesina–de Rugy ratio is today's Greece. Curiously, this research paper, published in March 2013, only mentions Greece in passing. Regardless of whether we are looking for evidence of spending-biased austerity per se, or for the merits of protracted periods of austerity, data from Greece over the past five years provide an excellent testing opportunity.

It could be objected that there is not enough time-series data to draw any decisive conclusions on Greece. This is a valid point. However, the same criticism could be used against most of the studies that Alesina and de Rugy base their conclusions on. Episodes of austerity are often no longer than 3–4 years, making it dicey to draw rigorous conclusion from them. Yet this happens often, ostensibly because mainstream-oriented economists are overly reliant on econometrics and harbor an under-appreciation of theory and analysis.

While, again, there is merit in the pro-austerity literature, and while it inspires to further research, there is also a universal discord between proponents and opponents of austerity. This discord has to do with the choice of goals for fiscal policy. Keynesians generally want their policies to lead to full employment. In order to defeat Keynesian theory, one therefore has to beat them at their own game. This means that a successful test of the anti-Keynesian hypothesis would have to establish that *during or immediately after the austerity policies are finished, employment is either higher than it was at the beginning of the crisis* (call this hard evidence) *or unemployment is in decisive and sustained decline* (soft evidence).

A reason why this is a necessary test can be found both in Sweden in the 1990s and in today's Europe. EU member states that have pursued austerity in recent years have notably higher unemployment now than they had before the crisis. In Greece, unemployment increased from 8.3 percent in 2007 to 24.3 percent in 2012; during the same period, Spanish unemployment went up from 8.3 percent to 25 percent; Portugal saw its unemployment climb from 8.9 to 15.9 percent.

Until there is credible evidence that spending-biased austerity can bring an economy to full employment (hard evidence) or put it on a trajectory toward full employment (soft evidence), skeptics of austerity—yours truly included—will maintain that the anti-Keynesian hypothesis has not yet been proven.

What are the broader consequences of this conclusion for economic policy and the role of government in our economy?

Austrians versus Keynesians: Can Theory Provide the Final Answer?

Since the anti-Keynesian hypothesis has not yet trumped Keynesian theory in terms of austerity, does this mean that Keynesian theory prevails as the stronger economic theory over Austrian theory? If so, does this mean that Keynesians who claim that government has a valid role in the economy are correct?

These questions are very important. In the general public policy arena there is an established wisdom, so to speak, that those who favor austerity are typically favorable to Austrian economics. In a similar fashion, modern-day Keynesians tend to oppose any kind of austerity and propose an active role for big government in the economy.

Both are wrong—and right. They both are wrong in assuming to have a complete answer to the economic crisis facing Europe today, but they are both right to enough of an extent that we can build an answer to the current crisis on both Austrian and Keynesian economics.

In order to build that remedy we first need to understand the merits and demerits of both theories. Beginning with Keynesianism, it is important that we understand what role it really ascribes to government. Its founder, British economist John Maynard Keynes, rarely spoke of government in his scholarly work. There are very few mentions of government in his most important contributions to economics, namely *A Treatise on Money* and *The General Theory of Employment, Interest and Money*. His most frequent references to government were in essays, written more to be polemical rather than analytical, such as "Can Lloyd George do it?" "Am I a Liberal?" or "The end of laissez-faire." However, in these essays he either advocated ad-hoc solutions to high unemployment, such as infrastructure investment, without providing an analytical backup of their merits; or speculated about the possible merger of interests between big corporations and government over the longer period of time. None of this can be construed as a serious attempt at scholarly analysis.

On that front, though, Keynes placed himself on the economics map in a major way with his *General Theory*. Based on this game-changing contribution to the foundation of macroeconomics, economists such as John Hicks and Paul Samuelson made significant strides to formalize and expand on Keynes's work.

One problem with the increased use of formal analysis, inspired by mathematics, is that followers or interpreters of Keynes focused so much on the "mechanics" of macroeconomics that they lost contact with his original theory. What was originally a depression theory, aimed at explaining why an economic depression occurs and what to do about it, was gradually transformed into a system with smooth mathematical properties but without some key elements that Keynes had relied on for his work.

This led to theoretical sacrifices, one of which was the limited role that Keynes saw government play in the economy. What emerged instead of Keynes's original work was a neat macroeconomic model, served today to economics students as the IS-LM model. This model conveniently lent itself to studies of an active role of government in the economy. It was easy for economics students with a keen interest in expanding government to find support for their big-government desire in what macroeconomics taught them.

Over time, Keynes's theory got "hijacked" by the political left, whose academic use of it rendered them a supposedly valid platform for scientifically establishing their beliefs in big government. Part of the blame for this falls on the shoulders of the recent tradition called post-Keynesianism. Spearheaded by primarily Sidney Weintraub and Paul Davidson, the post-Keynesian tradition originally sought to revive Keynes's legacy. However, their original ambitions were quickly run over by assorted statists who turned post-Keynesian economics into their own playground. Today, post-Keynesianism provides "scholarly" credibility to proponents of the Living Wage principle[6] or the backers of the idea that government should be some kind of employer of last resort.[7]

Rather than a big-government economist, Keynes was a depression economist. His main theoretical contribution is essentially an explanation of:

1.   how a recession can escalate into a depression;

2.   why economies get stuck in a depression; and

3.   how they can be brought out of the depression.

His theory rests on three pillars:

1.   *The multiplier.* Originally introduced by R.F. Kahn in 1931,[8] the multiplier is a centerpiece in Keynesian macroeconomics. It is a tool for identifying the "proliferation" of a change in economic

---

6   Please see: http://nakedkeynesianism.blogspot.com/2013/02/minimum-wage-and-unemployment-brazilian.html.

7   Tcherneva, P.R., "Permanent on-the-spot job creation – the missing Keynes plan for full employment and economic transformation," *Review of Social Economy*, Vol. LXX, No. 1, March 2012. Both this idea and the Living Wage hypothesis have been empirically disproven by the experiences from highly unionized economies with higher entry-level wages and higher unemployment than the United States; and by the failure of employer-of-last-resort programs in Europe.

8   Kahn, R.F., "The relation of home investment to unemployment," *Economic Journal*, June 1931.

activity, either positive or negative, throughout the economy. The most commonly used example of a multiplier effect is that when consumers suddenly have more money in their pockets, but over time the multiplier effect has increasingly been used in the context of increased government spending.

2.   *Uncertainty.* Keynes opens chapter 16 of his *General Theory* with an explanation of how effective demand begins to decline. When consumers and/or entrepreneurs go pessimistic they reduce effective demand; the reduction spreads through the economy via the multiplier; when the downturn reaches a critical mass over a critical period of time, consumers become overwhelmingly pessimistic.

3.   *The paradox of thrift.* This is a staple of Keynesian theory, saying simply that if all economic agents try to save themselves wealthy at the same time, then they are all going to get poor in the bargain. The reason is that in Keynesian theory there is no intertemporal price mechanism that equates the cancellation of consumption today to a promise to spend money tomorrow.

These three pillars constitute the core of Keynes's depression theory. The multiplier has been widely adopted in mainstream macroeconomics while uncertainty, the second pillar, is often neglected. This is unfortunate, because without it, it is difficult to understand Keynes's analysis of how depressions come about and how they persist. Keynes captured its role in the economy in the opening of Chapter 16 of *General Theory*:

> *An act of individual saving means — so to speak — a decision not to have dinner to-day. But it does not necessitate a decision to have dinner or to buy a pair of boots a week hence or a year hence or to consume any specified thing at any specified date. Thus it depresses the business of preparing to-day's dinner without stimulating the business of making ready for some future act of consumption. It is not a substitution of future consumption-demand for present consumption-demand, — it is a net diminution of such demand. Moreover, the expectation of future consumption is so largely based on current experience of present consumption that a reduction in the latter is likely to depress the former, with the result that the act of saving will not merely depress the price of consumption-goods and leave the marginal efficiency of existing capital unaffected, but may actually tend to depress the latter also.*

In this event it may reduce present investment-demand as well as present consumption-demand.

The pessimism that drives consumers to reduce spending today spreads to entrepreneurs, who in turn hold back on investments and employment. Or, in the succinct words of post-Keynesian economist Paul Davidson from his book *Money and the Real World*, "In a world of uncertainty, he who hesitates is saved to make a decision another day."

If the reduction in consumer spending appears to be of a regular kind, then businesses normally concentrate on keeping production capacity intact and get ready for the upturn. If on the other hand the reduction in spending is steep, fast and widespread, the recession will eventually escalate into a depression. The typical escalation process is one where the vast majority of households and entrepreneurs hesitate, that is, decide that it is better for them individually to save their money and their resources for another day. By being thrifty they hope to preserve, perhaps even grow their prosperity.

Paradoxically, their collective exhibition of individual rationality will have the exact opposite effect than they intended. A general decline in economic activity, due to an increase in the propensity to save, reduces sales revenues for private businesses; demand for labor declines, causing a drop in household disposable income. Consumer spending declines again, and the multiplier works its way through the economy.

The process from increased savings to declining prosperity is known as the paradox of thrift. It is important to understand that this paradox does not tell us that all savings are bad, nor does it tell us that consumers should spend everything they earn. Increased savings out of rising income is driven by a different motive than increased savings in tough economic times: the former is aimed to build prosperity over the long term, while the latter is aimed to preserve prosperity over the short term. The former is "offensive" while the latter is "defensive." The former reinforces an upward trend in economic activity, while the latter causes or reinforces an economic downturn.

Another, and for the topic of this book more important, application of the paradox of thrift has to do with austerity. Since, again, the welfare state does not operate in an economic vacuum, decisions to spend less money through entitlement systems do have consequences for the rest of the economy. When government is consistent enough in cutting spending, its actions will have negative consequences similar to those that follow a "defensive" rise in household savings.

As the savings rate rises in the economy in a recession, overall activity slows down further than it already has. From a Keynesian viewpoint, this is important with reference to the question of whether or not austerity is a workable policy strategy. The idea behind austerity—at least as it is expressed in the anti-Keynesian hypothesis—is that a reduction in the debt-to-GDP ratio will motivate consumers to spend more money and/or entrepreneurs to invest more. But if Keynesian theory is correct, then austerity is reinforced by consumer pessimism.

Since austerity has this depressing effect on consumer spending, does this mean that Keynesian theory refutes the anti-Keynesian hypothesis? To answer this question, let us sum up what we know thus far:

- during austerity consumers are bombarded with changes to government programs;

- they have become dependent on these programs for decisions on what to do with their disposable income from month to month;

- when government makes cutbacks to these programs, they experience a decline in their disposable income;

- their response is to either further reduce their spending or to endure on credit, hoping for "better days."

We can conclude from this that once the austerity period is over their confidence returns, hence the rise in spending. Thus, we have a Keynesian explanation of the evidence found by Giavazzi and Pagano (1995) regarding the correlation between protracted austerity and upturns in private consumption.

Does this mean there is no room for Austrian theory in the context of austerity? This is a valid, important question. In order to reach an answer, let us ask what role government actually plays in Keynes's depression theory.

The interpretation of Keynes's theory as implying a role for big government probably originates in the fact that governments in the United States and Europe used government outlays in various forms to spend their economies out of the depression. It is rather well established by now that those programs did not at all help toward a recovery, but that they actually prolonged the depression.[9] Furthermore, many of the spending programs that were put in place after the depression, often sold as preventative measures against future depressions, were actually pieces of a future welfare state. Instead of providing any kind of protection against a depression they added up to a permanent burden on the private sector, both in terms of its taxes and in terms of destructive incentives toward sloth, indolence and perennial government dependency.

Europe and North America alike climbed out of the depression despite, not thanks to, the expanding welfare states. At the time, government was small enough of a burden for the private sector to cope with, work around and incorporate into its operating costs. However, as the welfare state has grown over time the very same measures that were sold as the macroeconomic version of an anti-depression medicine have now brought the European economy to its knees.

In other words, history does not offer any good examples of how government could bring an economy out of a depression. There is a good reason for this: in order to restart the economy in a depression, government would have to significantly turn around consumer confidence; in order to turn around consumer confidence government would have to inject a sufficiently strong, sufficiently long-lasting volume of economic activity that would break consumer uncertainty. Both history and economic theory tell us that it is simply not possible for government to construct any program that can have such massively positive effects on consumer and entrepreneurial confidence.

The only form of government intervention that, hypothetically, could break down consumer uncertainty would be one that paid out large amounts of cash on a sustained basis, straight into the pockets of pessimistic consumers. However, such programs would have to come with such exceptionally destructive taxes that any positive macroeconomic effect one could expect from them would be ruined entirely by those taxes.

It is also worth noting that we already have such programs in place today, with large work-free transfers of money to tens of millions of Americans, and

---

9   A strong challenge to the notion of productive government anti-depression programs can be found in Shlaes, A., *The Forgotten Man: A New History of the Great Depression*, Harper Perennial, New York, 2008. A short piece on the same topic:

Fulsom, B. and Fulsom, A., "Did FDR end the Great Depression?" *Wall Street Journal*, April 12, 2010.

even more people in Europe.[10] The problem is that they did not prevent the deep recession we are currently experiencing.

If the entitlement programs of the welfare state could cure a depression, then surely they should be capable of preventing one as well.

Beyond the fact that government-provided, work-free income does not strengthen the economy it is worth asking: if government in general has a positive influence on economic activity, and if income redistribution protect us against economic slumps, then how is it possible that the entire industrialized world is so easily hurled into a recession as happened in 2008–09? How can a government that consumes nearly—or in some European countries more than—half of GDP be defeated by a wave of bank credit losses? If government is the answer to economic crises, then just how big must it grow before it can serve that role adequately?

Inevitably, our conclusion must be that an interventionist government cannot solve the problems associated with either a recession or a depression. This does not entirely rule out a government role in recovering an economy from a depression, but its role would have to be non-interventionist. That role would come with very different policy measures than those that modern Keynesians tend to suggest. By focusing on the management of so-called macroeconomic uncertainty, as opposed to microeconomic, or market-specific uncertainty, government can build an institutional framework that helps private businesses navigate an uncertain economy toward greater levels of confidence.[11] The norm-based policies put in place by the Bildt administration in Sweden in 1991–94 exemplify how government manages macroeconomic uncertainty.

Contrary to what conventional wisdom would say, Keynesian theory actually helps us explain why it is a bad idea to have a big government in the first place. While recessions are inevitable in a free-market economy, depressions as we know them are either caused or exacerbated by government. This is especially true with the current crisis, where austerity-minded

---

10 For an eye-opening study of how much welfare in the United States really pays, see: Tanner, M. and Hughes, C., *The Work vs. Welfare Trade-Off: 2013*, Cato Institute, Washington, DC, August 2013. Available at: http://www.cato.org/publications/white-paper/work-versus-welfare-trade, accessed February 3, 2014.

11 According to original Keynesian theory, there is a role for a non-interventionist government to facilitate the recovery of a depressed economy. For a detailed analysis, see: Larson, S.R., *Uncertainty, Macroeconomic Stability and the Welfare State*, Ashgate, London, 2002.

governments have spread uncertainty and pessimism among large segments of the population who depend on government, and where austerity measures have multiplied into much larger negative responses than often anticipated.[12]

In other words, the three pillars of Keynesian theory help us understand what role government can play in the economy:

1.   it can manage macroeconomic uncertainty but should stay away from intervening in the daily activities of the economy; and

2.   it should be so small that if our legislators try to close a budget deficit with austerity, the effects on the rest of the economy will be limited enough to prevent the paradox of thrift from going to work.

This way, government will not cause an acceleration of a recession into a depression, but instead leave the recovery phase to the free market.

At this point, we find ourselves at an intersection between Keynesian and Austrian theory. Just like Keynes built his theory partly on the inescapable presence of uncertainty in the economy, one of the most prominent figures in Austrian theory, F.A. Hayek, recognized that the economy is and will always be confined to operating under fundamental (aka macroeconomic) uncertainty.[13] This means two things. First, Austrian and Keynesian theory both recognize that free-market agents have limited information about the future; and second, business cycle fluctuations are inevitable, and there is always a risk that an economy will plunge into a depression.

It may seem like a trivial acknowledgement of the facts of the real world to admit that "yes, business cycles exist." But there is a surprisingly rich plethora of economic research that essentially tries to disregard or explain away business cycles. This often leads to forecasting errors in modern macroeconomic models, a point that Cato senior fellow Dan Mitchell has made repeatedly.[14] The main problem with modern economics in this respect is that it relies too much on

---

12   Blanchard, O. and Leigh, D., *Growth Forecast Errors and Fiscal Multipliers*, Working Paper 1301, International Monetary Fund, Washington, DC, January 2013.

13   For an innovative approach to Keynes, Hayek and uncertainty, see: http://www.kcl.ac.uk/sspp/ departments/geography/research/hrg/researchsymposium/2aBoy.pdf, accessed December 27, 2013.

14   This article makes his point well: http://danieljmitchell.wordpress.com/2013/01/27/dont-trust-economists-part-ii/, accessed December 27, 2013; for an earlier example, see: http://old. nationalreview.com/nrof_comment/comment-mitchell101802.asp, accessed September 2013.

technical tools and too little on analytical reasoning of the kind that Keynes and many Austrians engaged in.

While Austrian theory is in agreement with Keynesianism over the existence of uncertainty as well as its complex repercussions for economic activity, the two schools differ on especially one important point, namely the role of savings in the economy. This difference, which helps us further understand the role that government can play in the economy, was recently highlighted by British economist Robert Skidelsky in an explanation of how the two theory traditions saw the Great Depression:[15]

> For Hayek in the early 1930's, and for Hayek's followers today, the "crisis" results from over-investment relative to the supply of savings, made possible by excessive credit expansion. Banks lend at lower interest rates than genuine savers would have demanded, making all kinds of investment projects temporarily profitable. But, because these investments do not reflect the real preferences of agents for future over current consumption, the savings necessary to complete them are not available. They can be kept going for a time by monetary injections from the central bank. But market participants eventually realize that there are not enough savings to complete all the investment projects. At that point, boom turns to bust. Every artificial boom thus carries the seeds of its own destruction. Recovery consists of liquidating the misallocations, reducing consumption, and increasing saving. Keynes (and Keynesians today) would think of the crisis as resulting from the opposite cause: under-investment relative to the supply of saving – that is, too little consumption or aggregate demand to maintain a full-employment level of investment – which is bound to lead to a collapse of profit expectations.

Hayek's point about misallocated assets is highly important in the context of our modern, big welfare state. Because government operates outside of the free market, it excels at misallocating resources. In fact, the point has even more validity than just in reference to capital: it is just as important when it comes to income distribution. A dollar taken from Jack in the form of taxes and given to Joe in the form of an entitlement is a misallocation of current spending. It injects a wedge between work-free consumption and supply of labor that eventually

---

15 Please see: http://www.skidelskyr.com/site/article/the-keynes-hayek-rematch/, accessed December 27, 2013.

has negative effects on the economy similar to those observed by Austrians under a market-distorted interest rate.

For this reason we can extend Hayek's call for "liquidating the misallocations" to the "liquidation" of entitlement programs. The problem is that regardless of which liquidation we are talking about, if it is executed rapidly as some prescribe, its impact on the economy will be thoroughly negative.

This Keynesian conclusion does not constitute an argument against shrinking government. But it does constitute an argument against rapid, across-the-board spending cuts. Unfortunately, this point is missed on some Austrian economists, such as economics professor Phillip Bagus at the King Juan Carlos University in Madrid, Spain. In an essay from November 2012 for the Cobden Centre, Bagus puts Hayek's theory to work in today's Spain, focusing on government over-indulgence:[16]

> *Unfortunately, austerity is the necessary condition for recovery in Spain, the eurozone, and elsewhere. The reduction of government spending makes real resources available for the private sector that formerly had been absorbed by the state. Reducing government spending makes profitable new private investment projects and saves old ones from bankruptcy.*

The trick with cutting government spending is to avoid setting in motion a multiplier-driven paradox of thrift. The trick is also to recognize the role that uncertainty plays in the economy. Bagus does neither, which he clearly demonstrates with his illustration of how the liquidation of misallocated resources would turn the economy around:

> *Tom wants to open a restaurant. He makes the following calculations. He estimates the restaurant's revenues at $10,000 per month. The expected costs are the following: $4,000 for rent; $1,000 for utilities; $2,000 for food; and $4,000 for wages. With expected revenues of $10,000 and costs of $11,000 Tom will not start his business. Let's now assume that ... government closes a consumer-protection agency and sells the agency's building on the market. As a consequence, there is a tendency for housing prices and rents to fall. The same is true for wages. The laid-off bureaucrats search for new jobs, exerting downward*

---

16 Please see: http://www.cobdencentre.org/2012/11/the-myth-of-austerity/#, accessed December 27, 2013.

pressure on wage rates. Further, the agency does not consume utilities anymore, leading toward a tendency of cheaper utilities.

It is correct that even in highly unionized economies like the ones in the EU, high unemployment puts a downward pressure on wages. Therefore, Bagus is right in that the labor costs for Tom the Restaurateur will decline as a result of increased unemployment. His other two cost assumptions—a decline in rent and a decline in the price of utility services—seem a bit more dubious, but at least it is fair to assume that there will be no upward pressure on either of them.

However, let us assume that Bagus is right in that all production costs for Tom's restaurant will fall as a result of government closing an agency. As a purely theoretical experiment, his example proves that Hayek was right: liquidation of misallocated resources will help the economy recover.

The problem is not an axiomatically confined microeconomic cosmos. The problem lies instead in Bagus's assumption about revenue. The example is supposed to provide support for current austerity measures in Spain, and even argue for more of the same. But Spain is in a state of economic crisis, with 27 percent unemployment and a record of private consumption growth that—including 2013 and 2014 forecasts—is not exactly the kind that inspires entrepreneurial optimism:

Table 5.1   Spanish consumption

	2009	2010	2011	2012	2013	2014
Spanish consumption growth	-1.9	0.9	-0.8	-2.6	-3.2	-0.2

Source: Eurostat.

Assuming that the market for restaurant dinners develops in the same direction as overall consumer spending, it is reasonable to conclude that the market where Tom is planning to open his business is already over-populated with restaurants. Existing eateries have experienced stagnant or declining sales in recent years, with a downward pressure on dinner prices. What reason does Tom have to believe that he can out-compete existing businesses and even be within striking distance of making a profit or at least breaking even?

Let us make the problem even more tangible, and useful in the context of austerity. The costs to the restaurant that Professor Bagus mentions are usually highly predictable: landlords want a signed lease with a defined monthly rent; utilities want a fixed price per kilowatt of electricity, or a fixed monthly fee for internet and telephone services; the garbage collection company will want a contract with a clearly defined price for their regular services.

Even employees prefer reasonably predictable earning conditions, such as an hourly wage and an expectation of a certain number of hours per week. Even if wholesalers of raw materials for the restaurant would be flexible on their prices and how much to deliver each day, Tom's operating costs are going to be mostly fixed and essentially stay the same from one month to the next.

The same cannot be said about his revenues. In a tight market where there is already fierce competition between existing businesses, Tom will have a very hard time establishing a regular revenue stream with recurring patronage. The very least we can conclude is that due to a tight, declining market for restaurant dinners, his prospective revenues are more uncertain than the expected revenue stream for existing businesses—and far more uncertain than his costs of operation.

Lastly, we cannot ignore the fact that laid-off bureaucrats have less money to spend and therefore are less likely to come to anyone's restaurant and have dinner. Therefore, the larger the "liquidation of misallocated investments," the tighter demand will be for the very product on the market that Tom the Restaurateur wants to enter. Therefore, a more likely scenario than that Tom can benefit from a downward pressure on costs is that not only will he be unable to profitably enter the market, but the decline in restaurant patronage will put some existing restaurants out of business.

But all is not lost in Bagus's Austrian defense of austerity. He does have one point that opens for a successful economic recovery:

> *As the government has reduced spending it can even reduce tax rates, which may increase Tom's after-tax profits. Thanks to austerity the government could also reduce its deficit. The money formerly used to finance the government deficit can now be lent to Tom for an initial investment to make the former agency's rooms suitable for a restaurant. Indeed, one of the main problems in countries such as Spain these days is that the real savings of the people are soaked up and channeled to the government via the banking system. Loans are practically unavailable for private companies, because banks use their funds to buy government bonds in order to finance the public deficit.*

A minor point before we get to the useful part. The two first sentences are contradictory: the very purpose behind austerity is to reduce and eventually eliminate a deficit in the government budget. That cannot be done if government cuts spending and taxes at the same time. So long as the very goal with austerity is to close the budget gap, the tax cut that Bagus suggests cannot happen.

Now for the good news. If we redefine the purpose of austerity to reducing the size of government, then the spending cuts can be paired with strategic tax cuts. Unlike spending cuts at given taxes, where government keeps taking as much from the economy as it did before but returns less, the coupling of spending cuts to strategic tax cuts constitutes a permanent rollback of government in the economy. Government withdraws by using less resources (spending less) and returns purchasing power to the private sector (tax cuts) so that the private sector gets full room to replace government.

If the purpose behind Bagus's original spending cut—the closing of a consumer-protection agency—is to permanently shrink the size of government, not to close a budget gap, then the spending cut can be paired with, say, an income tax cut. The income tax cut, in turn, will put more money in the pockets of consumers and thus allow them to increase their demand for restaurant dinners.

At this point, Bagus's example becomes highly relevant. The decline in wages and prices that he uses as a vehicle for Tom to make his business proposal affordable now becomes a relevant part of the picture. The revenue side, which was questionable under the assumption that austerity aims to close a budget gap, now looks more credible.

Does this mean that Austrian theory trumps Keynesian theory in proposing a path to recovery? No, but it does not mean the opposite either. What we have here is a situation where Austrian and Keynesian reasoning both provide important insights into how to solve an economic problem. On the one hand, Austrians are right about government misallocating resources—a point that Keynesians notoriously ignore. If we extend this point to including income redistribution and its discrepancy between consumption and the supply of labor, then we have a very promising tool for gauging the size of economic adjustment needed to restore full employment.

An often-heard Austrian argument against expansionary monetary policy reinforces this point, namely that there are destructive downsides to an excessive supply of liquidity in the economy. They suggest, for example, that irresponsibly expansionary monetary policy will push interest rates too low and stimulate business investments beyond what would otherwise be profitable.

The mistake that Austrians often make in the context of excessive monetary expansion is that they tend to believe that an increase in private savings has a different effect on investments than an excessive money supply. But to the banking system, liquidity is always liquidity, and even though government-provided liquidity is more seductive than liquidity provided by private citizens it is unlikely that the borrower—the entrepreneur making the investment—is going to make a different decision if the low-cost liquidity he borrows originates in his neighbor's savings account or the central bank's monetary printing press.

The difference between expansionary money supply and expansionary private savings is that the former has no negative effect on consumer spending. When consumers increase their savings out of every $100 they make, they necessarily decrease their spending out of that same $100.

This is where Keynes comes in with the paradox of thrift: if we try to save ourselves rich we will end up poor. Again: my decision to save more instead of having dinner at Tom's Restaurant does not come with a promise to Tom's Restaurant that I will eat there tomorrow.

The trick, then, is to couple the highly valid Austrian argument about misallocation of resources with the Keynesian explanation of the multiplier and the paradox of thrift. One does not exclude the other. As an example of what this means, let us revisit Sweden. We will replace the austerity package of the 1990s with a very simple form of an Austrian-Keynesian synthesis.

What if Sweden Had Done Differently?

The Swedish 1990s austerity package was biased toward tax increases, raising taxes by 2 kronas for every 1 krona of spending cuts. The results as reported earlier were not very good from a macroeconomic viewpoint:

- the employment rate never returned to the levels of full employment during the 1980s;

- the per-taxpayer cost of the welfare state has gone up significantly and permanently; and

- households keep private consumption growing just above the industrial-poverty level by means of unsustainable borrowing.

The only successful outcome was an elimination of the government's budget deficit. Given the budgetary success and the macroeconomic failure, and given the suggestion in some of the austerity literature that a "flipped combo" of spending cuts and tax increases (i.e., two-for-one cuts versus tax hikes) would work better, let us test this combination on Sweden in the 1990s.

The two-for-one cuts package was suggested by Alesina and de Rugy. Their definition of success, however, is limited to a drop in the debt-to-GDP ratio, which makes it difficult to put their package up against the remarkable decline in Sweden's budget deficit reported in Figure 2.1 above. Therefore, to give Alesina and de Rugy a fair chance we should add macroeconomic success variables to the package, such as any two of the following three:

- increased private consumption;

- higher employment rate; and

- stronger GDP growth.

Before we proceed we need to acknowledge once circumstantial component that could make the Swedish situation different from the cases that Alesina and de Rugy use in their study. The Swedish 1990s austerity period began a couple of years after a massive depreciation of the currency. This depreciation de facto constituted a monetary expansion of considerable proportions, enough to make money very cheap, drive down prices of exports and turn a declining GDP into growth.

This puts the Alesina–de Rugy austerity package in the same problematic situation as was highlighted by Giavazzi and Pagano (1990). They downplay the results of their study based on the possibility that the changes to monetary policy that preceded austerity may have been the cause of an improvement in macroeconomic activity.

In Giavazzi and Pagano the monetary policy change established a fixed exchange rate combined with capital-flows liberalization; in the Swedish case the fixed exchange rate ended. While the macroeconomic stimulus coming out of the two policy changes differs—the fixed-rate policy stimulates private consumption and domestic investment while the flexible-rate policy stimulates exports—the end result is growth in job creation and an expanding GDP. Therefore, the Swedish case could present us with the same problems reported by Giavazzi and Pagano as we put the Alesina–de Rugy austerity package to work.

There is one way to neutralize the monetary policy effect, and that is to start implementing their simulated package at the same time as the actual package was implemented. This way we allow for the currency to depreciate and for the new exports boom to get underway; the actual and the simulated austerity packages are given the same circumstances.

Putting the Alesina–de Rugy package to work in Sweden not only allows us to give that particular combination of austerity policies a chance to prove itself, but it also opens for a limited application of our emerging Austrian–Keynesian synthesis:

- on the one hand, government misallocates capital and income, thus causing an over-utilization of economic resources in some areas and and under-utilization in others;

- on the other hand, a correction of this misallocation will, if done wrong, cause a downward spiral of economic activity due to the combined effects of the multiplier and the paradox of thrift.

Assuming that the deficit that Sweden experienced in the early 1990s was caused by government misallocating resources, we have two policy packages that represent two different strategies for, broadly speaking, correcting that misallocation. The Alesina–de Rugy package, downplaying tax increases, could be said to resemble a norm-based policy strategy in line with original Keynesian theory. In order to highlight this property of the package we will simply assume that there are no tax increases, and that the only spending cuts taking place are those that were included in the original package.

We could simulate a much larger spending-cut package, possibly as big as the total original package. However, that would require an intricate simulation process with changes to many variables that are now left constant. The quantitative work, while methodologically rigorous, would inject so many differences between the original austerity package and the simulated package that the results would be rather artificial. They would, in short, not yield enough unique output to validate the complexity of the input.

For this reason we will simulate the Alesina–de Rugy approach as consisting only of the spending cuts in the original austerity package.

Maintaining constant taxes is a form of norm-based policy. Therefore, if we assume that taxes were indeed kept constant in Sweden during the austerity years of 1995–98, then we effectively continue the same norm-based policies that were put in place as early as the fall of 1991. This norms-based strategy can also serve as a proxy for a Keynesian-based policy to manage macroeconomic uncertainty: by pledging to keep major economic variables unchanged over an extended period of time government reduces the individual firm's and household's exposure to risk, thus encouraging them to be a bit more optimistic and long-term oriented in their own economic activities. As consumer and entrepreneurial confidence grow, more money will be spent here and now, and more business investments will be made.

Technically, a continuation of the norm-based policies that keep taxes constant can be represented by a steady tax-to-GDP ratio. In 1994, the last year before austerity, that ratio was 47.9 percent in Sweden (not counting social security taxes). The actual austerity package increased this ratio to 51.5 percent by 1999, giving us a good view of how much more money the private sector would have kept under the simulated austerity package.

More specifically, the most important, from an economic viewpoint, tax increase was a new top income tax bracket. It was supposed to pull in a large part of the expected new tax revenues, namely 1.4 percent of GDP. Needless to say, this means that if the private sector had been allowed to keep that much money, Sweden would have experienced a notable rise in private consumption. This in turn would be good for our testing of the Alesina–de Rugy austerity package.

Two variables would dampen the rise in private consumption. The first is the propensity to import, that is, the share of every $1 of consumer spending that goes toward imported goods and services. The second has to do with the margin between what people receive in entitlements while out of work and what they take home on their first job after having been unemployed. In Sweden that margin is relatively small.

With these two dampeners in the picture, a straightforward estimate indicates that if the private sector had been allowed to keep the tax portion of the austerity package, private consumption would have increased enough to motivate a 1.5 percent annual employment increase.[17] If this rate had sustained during the austerity years, from 1995 through 1998, the Swedish economy would have enjoyed a 4.7 percent higher employment rate by 1998 than actual levels.

GDP would be notably higher, but not by as much as one might suspect. It is important to remember that when people are employed instead of unemployed they increase their spending by their propensity to consume out of the margin between their net-tax earnings and what they received in unemployment benefits (and other entitlements). This erodes the growth effect of reducing unemployment: an inflation-adjusted estimate points to GDP being 2.6 percent higher in 1998 under the simulation than under actual conditions.

With a higher GDP, the tax base expands. At a constant tax-to-GDP ratio the economy produces more tax revenues. A comparison between the rise in tax revenues under actual austerity and under the simulated Alesina–de Rugy package looks as follows (see Table 5.1).

Table 5.2   Actual and simulated tax revenue

	1995	1996	1997	1998
Actual tax revenue growth	6.5%	7.5%	5.1%	5.8%
Simulated tax revenue growth	8.9%	2.8%	5.2%	5.7%

Source: For actual tax revenue growth: Statistics Sweden, www.scb.se.

The actual, strong growth in 1995 is ostensibly attributable to the peak of an exports boom, following the sharp decline in the value of the krona in late 1992. It is expectable that this number would be higher in the simulation, as businesses take advantage of the continuation of the norm-based tax policy.

In 1996 the actual tax revenue increase substantially exceeds the simulated increase. This is, again, to be expected, as 1996 is the first year when the higher

---

17 This number is reached without the use of a formal macroeconomic model. The period of time studied is very short for a model to make much difference. The economic conditions preceding the austerity years are also rather unusual for an economy to be in, with massive unemployment, three years of shrinking GDP and an exceptionally large budget deficit. This makes modeling a risky project, as models are based on assumptions and observations of a long-term stable economy. For these reasons, the numbers presented here are reached through static calculations combined with a basic, Keynesian consumption function.

taxes have full effect in the actual scenario. By contrast the number in the simulated scenario displays their absence.

The large difference between actual and simulated revenue growth indicates that the exports boom was coming to an end at this point. As a consequence, the simulated scenario now relies entirely on the positive effects on domestic economic activity that would follow the sustained commitment to a norms-based fiscal policy. The higher tax-revenue growth numbers for 1997 and 1998 are good reasons to suggest that the norms-based policy would have had a sustained positive effect on economic activity.

At the same time, it is important to note that the actual scenario exhibited almost similar revenue growth numbers. The reason, again, is the massive and protracted increase in taxes.

The closeness between the growth numbers for 1997 and 1998 in both scenarios is in itself very telling. By leaving taxes unchanged, and by sticking to long-term fiscal policy norms, the Swedish government would have achieved an almost-as-fast reduction in its budget deficit as it actually did. (Remember that the spending cuts in the actual austerity package take place under the simulated package as well.) In fact, the accelerated increase in tax revenues in 1996–98 is a small exhibition of Laffer-curve effects:

- the actual austerity scenario increases tax revenues at a low employment rate, low growth and high taxes;

- the simulated scenario increases tax revenues as a result of growing employment, higher growth and comparatively lower taxes.

With a higher GDP and no tax increases under the simulated model, the Swedish government would have had almost exactly the same tax revenues in 1998 as it actually did when it raised taxes. It is therefore likely that a spending-cuts-only austerity package, one-third of the size of the actual package, under norm-based policies, would have reduced the budget deficit to the same extent as the actual austerity package did, but with:

- 186,000 more people employed, that is, another 4.7 percent of the total workforce that does not have to live on unemployment benefits;

- consumer spending 2.7 percent higher (adjusted for inflation); and

- a decline in dependency on entitlements that would have caused a more rapid decline in the budget deficit than assumed here.

The decline in demand for entitlements is not taken into account here because the spending cuts in the austerity package included changes to eligibility criteria for entitlements. There were also other changes made to entitlements during this period which overall make it a complicated task to estimate with reasonable accuracy just how big of an impact this would have on the budget deficit. A study of a longer period of time would give room for such calculations.

So, what conclusion can we draw regarding austerity and its usefulness in Europe today?

What are the lessons for the United States tomorrow?

Chapter 6

Way Forward

Let us take a step back and remind ourselves why we started this inquiry into industrial poverty. Europe has been in a long, stubborn economic crisis for five years now, with practically no end in sight. Most of the welfare states in the European Union exhibit similar signs of economic ailment: absence of GDP growth, stalled private consumption, large governments and high unemployment rates, especially among the young.

Policy experts and legislative leaders have teamed up to solve the crisis, but the policy measures they have used thus far have had no visible positive effects. If anything, they have aggravated the crisis. The reason for this is that austerity has the inherently negative effect of depressing economic activity. Today's big welfare states are far too intertwined with the private sector to allow large, invasive spending cuts without repercussions for private consumption, business investments and employment.

But there is a light in the tunnel. A carefully designed, strictly limited austerity package that excludes tax increases and is combined with a long-term oriented, norms-based fiscal policy could pave the way to success. The norms-based fiscal policy serves the purpose of building confidence among economic agents that the future is actually predictable enough for them to put some money to work.

The one caveat with this strategy is that the spending cuts must fall under the same norms-based principle as the tax policy does. One of the big problems with austerity in Europe today is that the private economy has been subjected to a series of seemingly never-ending spending cuts, changes to welfare eligibility, revised unemployment compensation rates, etc., all of which erodes confidence in the future. When households cannot foresee with good accuracy what they would have to live on, should they be unemployed, they will reduce spending today in order to make sure that they have enough in the bank should they lose their jobs. If this becomes the prevailing behavioral norm among consumers, the paradox of thrift kicks in and destroys any prospect of a better future.

If on the other hand spending cuts are reliably confined to clearly specified programs; if the changes to these programs are laid out well in advance; and if households can rely on those changes to be the only changes over the foreseeable future; then their response to the spending cuts could in fact be an increase in spending.

Deficits and Rolling Back the Welfare State

As currently used, spending cuts in Europe have been designed to preserve the welfare state. Legislators have wanted to reduce its cost to fit a shrinking tax base, but since their policies have in turn reduced the tax base their quest becomes a bad case of Sisyphean labor: they cut spending to reduce the deficit and slim-fit the welfare state, only to see the deficit grow again as the tax base shrinks.

Instead of focusing spending cuts on this fruitless endeavor, they should be designed to help boost macroeconomic activity. The last chapter showed how a limited, cuts-only austerity package could have made a difference for the better in Sweden. But the cuts must also serve another purpose, namely to permanently roll back the welfare state.

It is clear that the current crisis in Europe has its roots in the large welfare state. In order to avoid future eruptions of economic crises of the same magnitude and persistence, Europe's governments must therefore include yet another goal in their efforts to bring their economies up to growth again. That goal is a permanent roll-back of the welfare state.

If we are going to use spending cuts as part of a fiscal fight against a budget deficit, then we might as well design those cuts so that the size of government will not increase again. Better still, if the spending cuts are part of a long-term strategy to replace government services with privately provided services, then over time private-sector activity will grow even more strongly as boosted consumer and entrepreneurial confidence combine with investments in new markets.

Government's misallocation of economic resources is corrected without Keynesian macroeconomic repercussions.

How, then, would we put this theoretical platform to work? One example is free-market reforms in health care and health insurance. Suppose a country is in a recession with a budget deficit. One of its big spending programs is education. To open for free-market reforms government can make focused costs in two areas that do not affect the production of education itself: outlier functions, or functions that are farthest away from instructional activity; and outsourceable functions, or functions that are important to the daily operations of a school but are not instructional in nature.

By focusing on non-instructional functions, these cuts can—ideally—align a government operation with the operational principles of private businesses exposed to competition. When the same spending-cut principles are applied to all government operations, the accumulated reductions in government spending will give legislators a large enough austerity package to reduce the budget deficit and allow a norms-based tax policy to grow the economy.

Once GDP growth is under way there will be a surge in tax revenues. This allows for the next step in the privatization of entitlements, namely tax cuts designed specifically to give parents more purchasing power on a private education market. Since there is a plethora of literature on how to design such tax cuts (or tax credits, whichever is preferred) I shall not waste time on them here; the main idea is to sequence the phase-out of a government-run program, and to start the phase-out during a recession:

1.   *during the recession*: spending cuts that align government programs with the operational principles of private businesses;

2.   *simultaneous with spending cuts*: deregulation to allow private enterprises to compete with government;

3.   *as economy recovers*: tax cuts or other means of returning purchasing power to private citizens, allowing them to buy the services privately that government is in the process of privatizing.

The process toward full privatization obviously involves more steps, but these three steps are the ones that are relevant here.

Trimming government programs of excessive costs is a particularly good idea in an American context, where annual spending cuts are largely unknown. This reform principle can also be applied to other programs, such as income security.[1]

Free-Market Reforms and the Balanced Budget

One big obstacle to free-market reforms is a static political commitment to a government balanced budget. As far as Europe is concerned, current economic policy is not focused on anything else than to balance government budgets. The practical meaning of this is, needless to say, that governments are trying to recalibrate their welfare states to fit smaller tax bases. This recalibration in turn leads to a re-focusing of economic policy, away from full employment, onto the budget balance.

As we saw in the section about austerity, policy goals greatly influence the desired choice of policy measures. So long as focus is exclusively on balancing the government budget, legislators—American or European—will disregard any macroeconomic indicators that could show in which direction the economy is moving. This is the reason why blind focus on a balanced budget has hurled many European countries into a downward spiral of stagnation, doom, gloom and industrial poverty.

A more dynamic approach to policy goals would greatly help Europe recover, as well as help the United States avoid repeating the European crisis scenario. The combination of roll-back-oriented spending cuts, aimed at opening for privatization of government programs, and norms-based fixing of taxes is one way of aligning several policy goals: a balanced budget, economic growth, lower unemployment and reduced government. The only adjustment needed compared to the European, static approach to a balanced budget is a dynamic approach where the goal to eliminate the budget deficit is stretched out over a number of years rather than forced upon the budget annually.[2] The Swedish example gives us an idea of how this could work. We could draw similar information from the studies surveyed by Alesina and de Rugy, though with the caveat that those studies do not set the same policy goals as we do here.

---

1   Larson, S.R., *Ending the Welfare State: A Path to Limited Government That Won't Leave the Poor Behind*, Outskirts Press, Denver, 2012.
2   Compact for America has suggested an interesting balanced-budget amendment with dynamic mechanisms: http://www.compactforamerica.org/, accessed December 27, 2013.

In addition to combining several desirable policy goals under one umbrella, the Austrian–Keynesian synthesis discussed in Chapter 5 would also help bring about more stability to the economy. One of the major drawbacks of how austerity has been executed in Europe over the past few years is that it has greatly upset economic stability. Frequent, often panic-driven changes to taxes and entitlements have caused ripples of uncertainty throughout the economy, setting in motion a paradox-of-thrift style decline in private-sector activity. The more frequently government raises taxes and cuts spending, the more difficult it becomes for businesses to predict their future.

As a remedy, Europe needs the stability and predictability that comes from keeping taxes intact and launching a well-defined and long-term predictable package of spending cuts. But this is a learning experience for the United States as well: we have not yet reached the point where overwhelming fiscal panic sets in and defines the day on Capitol Hill and in the White House. That day, however, is not far away and will have thoroughly negative effects on our country's economy. In order to avoid it, and in order to avoid being dragged down into the same whirlpool of industrial poverty as Europe, our elected officials must devise a concise, forward-looking strategy to:

- bring the deficit under control;

- reduce permanently the spending obligations of the federal government;

- ease the regulatory burden on the economy;

- open more sectors of the economy, currently under government monopoly, to private competition;

- cut the tax burden on businesses and households; and

- redirect government from its current growth path toward its economically sound, limited functions.

Index

For Product Safety Concerns and Information please contact our EU
representative GPSR@taylorandfrancis.com Taylor & Francis Verlag GmbH,
Kaufingerstraße 24, 80331 München, Germany

Printed and bound by CPI Group (UK) Ltd, Croydon, CR0 4YY
08/05/2025
01864518-0001